Pastor, Counselor and friend —
He was all of these things to
this church and community — and
he loved you with unconditional
love! So do I!

Freddie
7/30/01

TOGETHER WITH GOD—A Journey
Through Grief

WILLIAM CLIFFORD MASON, JR.
"Happy Chappy"
1925-1990

TOGETHER WITH GOD—

A Journey Through Grief

By

Laura Lee Mason

With a Foreword by

Bishop Earl G. Hunt, Jr.

Granny Lavender Press

EMORY UNITED METHODIST CHURCH

Copyright © 2001 by Laura Lee Mason
All rights reserved.

For information address Granny Lavender Press
33325 Graceland Lane
Glade Spring, Va. 24340

ISBN: 0-9627706-2-0

Printed in the United States of America

DEDICATION

To W. C.

Whose life and ministry I was privileged to share and whose legacy of unconditional love continues to brighten the world in which he lived.

And

Bill, Linda, Ken, Ann, Peggy,
Laura Ruth, Zachary
and
The memory of Jonathan

Who provided enabling support and love as we traveled through this journey of grief.

CONTENTS

LETTER TO THE READER 9
PREFACE 11
INTRODUCTION 17
ACKNOWLEDGEMENTS 21
FOREWORD 25
CHAPTER I—THIS CAN'T BE HAPPENING TO ME 29
CHAPTER II—CELEBRATING A VICTORIOUS LIFE 37
CHAPTER III—THE STRUGGLE FOR SURVIVAL 45
CHAPTER IV—FRANTIC ACTIVITY OR PURPOSEFUL ENDEAVOR ... 53
CHAPTER V—YEARNING FOR THE PAST 59
CHAPTER VI—ENABLING SUPPORT, ENABLING LOVE 67
CHAPTER VII—THE FEARS, THE DOUBTS, THE FRUSTRATIONS .. 73
CHAPTER VIII—THE ANGER, THE GUILT, THE "WHAT-IFS" 79
CHAPTER IX—WORK ETHIC OR WORKAHOLIC? 85
CHAPTER X—SPECIAL DAYS—A YEAR OF "FIRSTS" 93
CHAPTER XI—I'M BEGINNING TO HEAL 103
CHAPTER XII—DOES GOD ANSWER PRAYER? YOU BET! 111
CHAPTER XIII—DESPITE NEW GRIEF, HEALING GOES ON 119
CHAPTER XIV—HAS GOD ABDICATED HIS POSITION
  OF POWER? 125
CHAPTER XV—EMBRACING WIDOWHOOD. 133
CHAPTER XVI—THANK YOU, GOD 139
SOURCE NOTES 145
WORKS CONSULTED 148

W. C. AND LAURA LEE (FREDDIE)

LAURA LEE, ANN, LINDA, BILL, W.C.

W. C. with his Grand-
children—

Above—Laura Ruth and
Zachary Davis.

To the Right—
Jonathan Anderson

Letter To The Reader

Dear Reader,

This book is written with the hope that it will help those who are dealing with grief. Though major emphasis is placed upon the elderly because this is where my grief experiences began, I think that the book will have universal appeal. Grief isn't restricted to any age or any particular circumstance.

The joys and struggles of the senior years are as much a part of our life experience as those of any other phase through which we traverse. One of the greatest fears couples face as they look toward these years is the growing awareness that the marvelous journey they embarked upon as newlyweds will probably not last a lifetime for both of them. Another wonderful journey is ahead, yes, and while faith helps us anticipate that new adventure, there is usually a period of time that separates us from our loved one before we can be reunited forever.

The excruciating experience of grief must be faced and lived through. What a blessing it is to know that, together with God, we can find light at the end of that terrible tunnel!

The utter devastation, confusion and frustration of my existence after the death of my husband were overwhelming. I thought my world had ended. I'm glad that God knew differently!

This book is an account of my sojourn with Him through a pilgrimage that brought me out of the depths of despair into the realization that life could, indeed, be good again. It is my fervent hope that out of my grief will come help for those who are experiencing this life-shattering, all-consuming phenomenon. In addition, it is my earnest desire for the legacy of my husband, W. C. Mason, Jr., to be passed on to student generations at Emory & Henry College who will never get to know him as a personal friend!

Because words are often inadequate I have included pictures that are not usually found in a book on grief. In addition to its primary purpose, I want *TOGETHER WITH GOD—A Journey Through Grief* to be a tribute to my husband who served The Holston Conference of The United Methodist Church and Emory &

Henry College with enthusiasm and integrity. I beg your indulgence and hope that the pictures will bring you into the intimacy of our family circle. Perhaps they will also help you identify with our struggles and with our joys—the kinds of struggles and joys that come to all of us somewhere along the way!

I am not an expert on grief. I am, however, an average person who has gone through the debilitation of grief that thousands of average persons face each year. Though I have no formal study of this area, I *do* have a practical knowledge, born of the necessity of coming to grips with grief in all of its ramifications. I have had searing encounters with the grief process. Within a period of ten years I lost six close family members, in addition to my husband! And after this manuscript was completed, my sixteen-year-old grandson was killed when he was hit by a train, thrown beneath its wheels and horribly mangled. I feel that my excruciating journeys through grief have given me insights that no textbook could provide. They have also enabled me to write with authenticity.

God has provided strength and courage as we sojourned through the ups and downs of these grief processes. With His help I have found healing. I have also regained meaning and purpose for my life. I know now that my destiny does not lie in the ashes of yesterday, as wonderful as yesterday was. It lies, instead, just ahead, and the prospects are exciting!

If you are reading this book because you are hurting, I pray for God's presence in your life. May you come away from its pages with the conviction that God will not desert you or give up on you. Look to Him for guidance and sustenance. Give Him a chance to heal your hurts!

Sincerely,

Laura Lee Mason

Laura Lee Mason

PREFACE

Very early in life, as a youngster of seven or eight, I felt the love of God reach down and touch my soul. It was at a tent revival in the city of New Orleans, Louisiana, and to my childish mind, Sister Grace, in her long flowing white gown, was the embodiment of Jesus Christ himself! Though I knew nothing about John Wesley at the time, I, too, "felt my heart strangely warmed!"

It was much later, in my teen years, that I felt the call of God to Christian service. That's when I met the person who would become my lifelong companion. I was in college preparing for work in the field of religious education. He was a fledgling minister in The Methodist Church, serving a student pastorate as he pursued studies leading toward seminary enrollment. We fell in love—hopelessly, helplessly and wonderfully! I accepted his proposal of marriage without hesitation. I wasn't abdicating my commitment to God; I was embellishing it! Where else could I possibly be of greater service? I felt then, as I do now, many decades later, that God was looking with favor upon this marriage.

After completing our studies at Tennessee Wesleyan College in Athens, Tennessee and Emory & Henry College in Emory, Virginia, we went on to Atlanta, Georgia where he enrolled in the Candler School of Theology. W. C.'s student pastorates included North Liberty Church and the Etowah and Shouns Circuits in the Holston Conference and the Marietta Circuit, Vinings-Pleasant Hill Charge and assistant to the pastor of Patillo Memorial Church in the North Georgia Conference.

After seminary we started our itinerant ministry in the Holston Conference of The United Methodist Church, our first pastorate being South Bristol on the Tennessee side of the twin city of Bristol. Four years later W. C. was sent to State Street as the associate pastor of this Bristol, Virginia church. Three years later he became the chaplain of Emory & Henry College and pastor of the Emory Methodist Church. It was there that W. C. Mason, Jr. became an "institution!" Dubbed "Happy Chappy" by his students, he went about entrenching himself in the hearts and lives of all who had occasion to know him. Students flocked to his office in droves to talk over a problem or just sit and chat with this man who had a ready smile and a penchant for strawberries and ice cream. While waiting their turn they helped themselves to pennies from the basket by the bubble gum machine and enjoyed a tasty chew—and when they came to his house, they anticipated getting to share his favorite dessert.

He continued to serve the College as he became dean of students, professor of religion and family life education and finally, director of campus religious life. In this capacity he developed an ecumenical resource center for religious education. He also maintained a marriage counseling service. During his tenure at Emory & Henry he pursued graduate studies at Boston University, the University of Southern California and New York University, receiving his doctorate from NYU in counseling.

The years slipped by as we went about our lives, enjoying the hectic but invigorating pace. Before we knew it, W. C. was approaching retirement and I had already stopped work to concentrate on responsibilites at home. I missed teaching weekday kindergarten at Emory and working with

People Incorporated Head Start; but with retirement came a freedom to be there for my elderly mother and aunt, whom W. C. affectionately referred to as his "girls." I also had more time to help him with the entertainment of students in our home.

Though we had dealt with experiences throughout our married lives that were hard, sometimes even devastating, I had not thought much about grief. In my mind, grief was something that usually came to other people. It was vague, general, hazy, and, oh yes, random. This complacent attitude pretty much summed up my feelings, until grief hit me with a double whammy! Denial—you bet!

We were in the forty-third year of a fantastic marriage and were serving a fulfilling ministry. The children and grandchildren had been home for Christmas, joining my elderly mom and aunt who lived with us, and my mother-in-law, who was visiting. A week later we joyously celebrated the promising New Year with close friends. Two months into that year I wrote in my journal, "God is in His Heaven and all is well with my world!"

And then the bomb exploded—the bomb that rained destruction on that safe little world and threatened to undermine my very faith in God *and* His Heaven. My lovable, warmhearted, cheerful, vigorous, dynamic husband was stricken with a fatal heart attack and died without regaining consciousness!

Grief was no longer random, hit or miss, general. It erupted violently into my space and thus became an intimate, intensely personal, unrelenting companion. Webster defines grief as "a deep mental anguish, as over a loss: sorrow." But grief *really* defies any attempt to describe it or spell out its meaning in full. It had invaded my life, however, and the effort to understand and deal with it was compelling.

W. C.'s death was a devastating blow! In another hour we would have been on our way to Chattanooga where he was scheduled to preach the next day. Within that short span of time, life as I had known and loved it was obliterated. I lost the person who meant more than life itself to me. My reality no longer included retirement years with him, a period of time I had looked forward to with great anticipation. An identity crisis loomed ahead as the pivotal point of my entire existence was snatched away without warning. I had interests and responsibilities of my own, of course, but they had always been secondary to being W. C.'s wife and helpmate. They were secondary because that was the way I *wanted* them to be!

Without warning I was thrown into the throes of grieving, not for W. C., but for myself. I called on God for help, knowing that if I asked for and expected to receive strength to face this tragedy, it would be granted. God's presence was real in my life. It didn't stop the tears, it didn't negate the heartache. It simply enabled me to face each day in the grief process with the assurance that "this, too, shall pass," and that one day meaning, purpose and even a measure of happiness would replace the utter devastation, confusion and frustration of my new existence.

I kept a notebook with me at all times, jotting down thoughts, insights, reflections and meditations as they came to me, sometimes in the wee hours of the morning. I read everything I could find on grief and life after death. I talked to professionals. I sought counseling. I truly yearned to be whole again.

At some point in time the realization came to me that death and grief are universal experiences. If we live long enough they will touch our lives. I wanted people who were going through this process to know that there would be devastation. I wanted them to understand that others also experienced the emotions they were experiencing, though no two people go through the grief process in exactly the same way. I wanted to urge them to get their feelings out in the open so they could deal with them and free themselves to go on living. And I wanted them to realize that the choices they made would determine the length and outcome of their grief process. Healing was within their grasp; they, too, could survive!

So I announced to my children that I was going to write a book on grief. Bill and Linda were enthusiastic—*well*, maybe accepting might better reflect their mood. My youngest daughter, Ann, who has the sometimes-alarming knack of saying exactly what she thinks, replied reflectively, "What do you know about grief that hasn't already been written?" She had me there, but I still felt compelled to try. I didn't come up with anything new. I didn't come up with anything different or earth shaking. What did emerge was an account of my walks with God through these sojourns and my deliverance on the other side.

I did not attempt to write a study of grief. There are many excellent books in the market that cover this aspect of the subject. I felt, however, that, as a novice, a student, a disciple, a layperson, if you will, I had been traveling an unknown road and making some important personal discoveries. I wanted to share these God-given insights with persons who are now, or who might someday, find themselves on this same journey.

This book is simply an attempt to sort through the thoughts and actions that were mine during those struggling years—the shock, the heartache and despair, the anger and regret, the fear. It is also about faith, acceptance and hope—peace, gratitude and love—discovery and growth. Unlike the seesaw movement of predictable ups and downs, these emotions made my journey through grief erratic. Forward steps were shaken by setbacks. I didn't go through this process in a methodical and systematic fashion. My grief was not rational; it was not logical; it didn't take one well-ordered step after another leading to its final cessation and a storybook ending. Perhaps it *will* end someday, I don't know. But I rather suspect that there will continue to be times of regression. I know, however, that there is a light at the end of the tunnel, for I have experienced its warmth and its glow.

Life will never be the same; life is at times unfair. But life is also good, if we allow it to be. Though others can help, no one can go through grief for us. The marvelous thing is that we don't have to travel this agonizing journey alone. God has promised us grace and strength sufficient for any task! It is ours for the asking.

W. C. AT AN OFFICE PARTY COMMEMORATING THE 39TH ANNIVERSARY OF HIS EMPLOYMENT AT EMORY & HENRY COLLEGE. HOW ASTUTE OF HIS CO-WORKERS TO PROVIDE A STRAWBERRY CAKE!

Introduction

All of us, to some degree or other, experience grief. It may not be caused by the death of a family member. The loss may not even occur through death. There can be loss of respect, loss of esteem, loss of communication, loss of health, loss of love, loss of a job, loss of a mate through divorce. Our children may be lost to the drug culture or alcohol or through yielding to the many temptations young people face as they navigate the teen and even the pre-teen years on their way to responsible adulthood.

And what about the loss of security as jobs are changed, the loss of friends and familiar surroundings with the move from one house to another, from the old neighborhood to the new, which might be thousands of miles away? Things are not the same. We grieve for what used to be before we can accept our new possibilities. The agony is real, the heartache a source of great anxiety and distress.

In talking about what she and her students have learned through their Seminars on Death and Dying, Elizabeth Kübler-Ross, society's preeminent authority on this subject, has listed five steps through which dying patients go as they cope with terminal illness. These steps have come to be recognized, also, as stages of grief through which persons traverse as they experience the loss of something or someone vital to their happiness and well-being. They are:

1. *Denial*—A temporary state of shock, disbelief and fear that makes us unable to face the facts. This can't be happening, we think. Denial acts as a buffer, giving us time

to gradually recuperate. Denial is never total and, as the feeling of numbness begins to disappear, it is replaced by partial acceptance.

2-*Anger*—Anger, rage, envy and resentment at people in our environment and at God replaces, and at times coexists, with denial. "Why me?" we ask.

3-*Bargaining*—We attempt to enter into an agreement with God which might possibly postpone the inevitable.

4. *Depression*—A sense of great loss, dismay, sadness, and hopelessness may bring on deep depression and a yearning for things to be normal again. Sometimes unrealistic guilt or shame accompanies depression.

5-*Acceptance*—As fear and despair diminish and finally disappear, we find ourselves able to reenter life and accept its changes. We often become more self-sufficient and independent in the process.[1]

"The one thing that usually persists through all of these stages is hope," states Dr. Kübler-Ross.[2] Aren't we fortunate that we can hold on to that hope?

Other authorities on grief have listed stages that differ somewhat, but retain the basic concepts. Granger Westburg, in his book, *Good Grief*, divides his steps into ten. They are:

1-*Shock*—A temporary numbness or stupor comes over us, making it possible to avoid facing total reality.

2-*Emotional Release*—We are able to express the emotions we feel, whether openly or in private, rather than bottling them up.

3-*Depression and Loneliness*—We sink into depths of despair, which may lift suddenly or may last for many months.

4-*Physical Symptoms of Distress*—We experience illness, which is brought on by unresolved grief.

5-*Panic*—Concentration is difficult; we become paralyzed with fear of the unknown; we want to run away from life.

6-*Guilt*—Real or neurotic feelings of guilt bother us until they are faced and resolved.

7-*Anger and Resentment*—These emotions will probably surface and be a source of pain until we accept the fact that they are both normal and acceptable.

8-*Resisting Returning*—We resist reentry to life because it is too painful to face our new, unpredictable world.

9-*Glimpses of Hope*—We experience glimpses of hope that help us realize life can be meaningful again.

10-*Affirming Reality*—We accept the fact that life will never be the same, but affirm its worth and reenter as a stronger person.[3]

Knowing about the stages of grief was helpful to me as I struggled to understand what was going on in my life. Seeking professional help was just the boost I needed to push me from one step to another on this bewildering journey.

Private counseling or group therapy sessions are invaluable, and they can be available at little or no cost. Churches, synagogues, funeral homes, hospices, hospitals and mental health facilities often sponsor grief support groups. Chaplains, rabbis, priests, pastors and therapists are trained to provide counseling on an individual basis. Needing help carries no shame; on the contrary, it is a wise person who sees this need in their life and takes steps to assure that it is met.

Grief is a personal experience. We do not all reach the same stage in a given amount of time. We may not even go through every step. Sometimes we find ourselves in more than one stage simultaneously, and there are even times when we revert to a level that we thought we had moved out of for good. Though its pattern, as set forth by authorities, might not precisely fit our own grief journey, it is good to realize that the frightening emotions we are encountering are normal. They are not only vehicles through which healing can come, they are feelings that must be dealt with on an ongoing basis if healing is to ensue. No longer do we need to doubt our sanity as we attempt to endure the losses that have thrown us into our own grief abyss. God has provided a way to help us cope—a step by step progression through which we can find wholeness. But, we have to work at it. We must *choose* to be whole again.

THE CHAPEL AT EMORY & HENRY COLLEGE

THE OFFICES AND FELLOWSHIP HALL IN MEMORIAL CHAPEL WERE NAMED FOR W. C. AND DEDICATED TO HIS MEMORY.

ACKNOWLEDGEMENTS

I am indebted to Bishop Earl G. Hunt, Jr., who reviewed my manuscript with an eye toward biblical and theological accuracy and made suggestions that greatly enhanced the finished product. I am both honored and delighted that he has also written the foreword. The Hunts and Masons arrived together at Emory & Henry College in 1956, Dr. Hunt having been assigned to the presidency of the College. We enjoyed a close relationship and our friendship continued after he was elected to the episcopacy. Bishop Hunt and his wife, Mary Ann, were supportive of me during the turbulent months following W.C.'s untimely death. I am, indeed, grateful to both of them.

Deep appreciation also goes to several persons who painstakingly checked the manuscript at various levels of revision for errors—Dr. Daniel G. Leidig, Mrs. Louise Fachilla, Mrs. Dorothy Culberson, Ms. Georgeanna Driver, Mrs. Jean Bartlett and Mrs. Nancy Griffin. Help with photography and graphic arts was provided by Mrs. Alice Dow, Mr. Jack Cox, Ms. Monica Hoel and Mr. Robert Vejnar and with computer technology by Mrs. Joy Dunbar.

I am grateful for the counsel of our friends and fellow ministerial couple, Dr. Bill Balch and his wife, Carol, who helped me think through some of my positions. I am thankful for my wonderful mom who was there for me every minute of every day until her death two years later and to my children and grandchildren, who continue to be a source of comfort and strength. I am also thankful for my sister, Joy, and her husband, Bud, and to W. C.'s mom, his brother, Glenn, and his wife, Margaret.

Chaplain Hal Hartley, his wife, Donna, and daughter Rebecca had become like family to us during the short time he and W. C. were privileged to work together. He was there for me night and day and was instrumental in helping me survive those first days and months of this grief journey.

And how could I have gotten along without the cadre of other close friends—Dot and Connie Culberson, Iris and Neel Rich, Ruby Graybeal, Georgeanna Driver, Ruth Biggers and Jean Bartlett? They were there for me from the very beginning and continue, to this day, to keep me in their care.

As this journey through grief progressed, other mentors came into my life providing additional nurture. I am deeply grateful to Chaplain David St. Clair and his wife, Marcia, who continued to support me as I went through the ups and downs of the grief process and to Rev. Brian Miller and his wife, Mary, Rev. Kathie Wilson-Parker and her husband, Bill, and Rev. James Bennington who was one of the students who showered love and care on me at the time of W. C.'s death and is now my beloved pastor.

Appreciation is also expressed to my publisher and editor, Dr. Terry R. Griffin, who has worked enthusiastically and tirelessly giving me suggestions for improvement and getting this manuscript into publishable form, and to his wife, Nancy, who was W. C.'s able and dedicated Administrative Assistant for many years.

As this manuscript went from publisher to publisher and through several sources of evaluation, I would beg God to show me where to send it next. In my devotions and in my reading, "God's timing" kept coming up and I finally turned my intense desire for publication over to Him. I continued to send it out, always with the hope and the prayer that God's timing would materialize. I should have been praying, also, for the ability to recognize it when it came!

With Dr. Griffin's offer to publish a collection of my children's stories, my efforts, for the moment, were redirected. Quite by accident, he discovered that I had written this manuscript on grief, and the rest is history!

What a joy it is to sit around the kitchen table with one's editor and publisher who is also one's long time friend! And how wonderful it is to work with someone who is not only extremely knowledgeable about what he is doing but is also truly excited about your efforts!

I wonder how long God was prodding me on to the discovery that His timing had, indeed, arrived! I am truly thankful that He didn't give up on me and that He stayed with me through the journey *and* through the process of relating it to others!

No one will ever convince me that God doesn't answer prayer!

EARL G. HUNT, JR.

RETIRED BISHOP OF
THE UNITED METHODIST CHURCH

Foreword

READING the manuscript of this book was an extraordinarily moving experience for me. Dr. and Mrs. W. C. Mason, Jr. went to Emory & Henry College at the same time my wife and I began our relationships to this historic institution. Our friendship developed and deepened across the years, and there are few people in my personal pantheon of heroes and heroines whom I regard as highly as I do W. C. and "Freddie" Mason. But my admiration of this poignantly realistic study of human grief and the victory that can be won over it is not based upon the subjective relationship which the Hunts have had with the Masons for such a long time. It has a far more solid and objective foundation.

The often excruciating agony of Mrs. Mason's odyssey through the wilderness of her sorrow is described with devastating honesty. Her candor will quickly discover responsive chords in the experience of readers who have endured similar pain. She writes in such vivid detail about her own struggles that any one of us who has lost a loved one can relate almost instantly to the grim contour of her despair. When she begins to emerge from her "dark night of the soul," the slow, often uncertain progress of her spiritual recovery fashions, at first dimly and then ever more brightly, the shape of a new hope which is at times elusive but always authentic. All through the book the author's careful analysis of her experience is creative and provocative, a point well illustrated by her exploration of the "stages" of widowhood.

Although the book is about the grief of his wife, the portrait of her husband is almost incredibly accurate and beautiful. William Clifford Mason, Jr. was one of God's noblemen. Committed totally to Christian liberal education, he understood the many faceted mystique of the small college with its students and faculty better than any person I ever knew. For thirty-four years, his well-furnished mind, effervescent sense of humor, indefatigable energy, deep Christian faith, and inexhaustible love of human beings made him a living legend on the lovely Emory & Henry campus; and when he died so suddenly, he took his place forever among the immortals in the history of this famous old institution in Southwest Virginia. Mrs. Mason captures with delightful, sometimes droll humor the delectable eccentricities of her husband until the image of his personality and character emerges in a way that defines both the depth of their marriage and the integrity of her grief.

This book is highly readable. Indeed, when the author sent me her manuscript, I completed my own initial perusal of it in a single sitting. Her easy flow of English is natural and graceful, and the fascinating manner in which she tells the story of her experiences quite literally captivates the reader. This is neither an academic nor a physiological examination of the anatomy of grief, but rather the practical diary of a sensitive person who has passed through its terrible darkness. Incidentally, she has buttressed her story with appropriate quotations from a select company of others who have dealt with the theme of bereavement and have spoken helpfully about it.

It must be very hard to write an honest book about human sorrow. Particularly is this so if the author is a person of deep religious conviction. One temptation surely would be to find light at the end of the tunnel too quickly and readily.

Foreword

The person whose mature faith has been hammered out on an anvil of life's tragic vicissitudes knows that doubt is real and can be persistent. There is a long, long trail from tragedy to triumph. This book walks the entire length of that trail. I have only encountered two such works which I should not hesitate to pass on to men and women who have experienced shattering human grief. This is one of them.

I heartily commend *TOGETHER WITH GOD—A Journey Through Grief* to all those who would turn sorrow into hope and lay fresh hold upon the Christian doctrine of Life Eternal.

Earl G. Hunt, Jr.

EMORY & HENRY COLLEAGUES
DR. DAN LEIDIG, MR. FRED ENTLER, MR. G. C. CULBERSON
PRESIDENT EARL HUNT, W. C.

CHAPTER I

THIS CAN'T BE HAPPENING TO ME!

"I called upon the Lord in distress; the Lord answered me, . . ."
(Psalm 118: 5)[1]

THE terrifying thud of my husband's head hitting the door as he collapsed will remain with me always. The vacant look in his eyes, the cries of the child within him for his mother—his only utterances—and the shallow breathing of my comatose mate left me little doubt that our marriage was nearing an end. "Till death us do part," ominous words from our long ago wedding vows, were about to become a devastating reality.

I tried frantically to breathe life into his body. I held him close, pillowed his head in my lap, and begged him not to leave me.

Off in the distance I heard my Aunt Ethel call the Life Saving Crew. I was grateful that she was there. Donna, our chaplain's wife, arrived and took over the resuscitation efforts while her husband, Hal, ran out to direct the paramedics. The wail of the ambulance, the efforts of crew members to revive W. C., and the trip to the hospital with loving and supportive friends is still a haze in my memory. I don't know who gave the information to the emergency room clerks. Neither do I

---

[1]Scripture quotations not otherwise identified are from the King James Version of the Bible.

know how long we waited while W. C. hovered between life and death. I do remember with agonizing clarity the dreadful realization that he would not survive.

"He's dying, Hal, he's dying," I kept repeating, and I knew, even before they called us into the room to talk with the attending physician, that he was gone.

"I'm sorry. We did everything we could," the doctor said. "It was too late."

Too late, my thoughts raced on. Why didn't the Life Saving Crew get there sooner? Why didn't our efforts to revive him succeed? Why didn't I think to call our community doctor and our campus security personnel? Too late, surged through my consciousness again and again; it *can't* be too late! But I knew instinctively that it had been too late by the time his body had hit the floor.

My world was spinning around, but I seemed to be detached from it. This can't be happening to me, I agonized through the trance that had penetrated my being. I heard someone ask if I wanted to see W. C. and a quick *no* escaped my lips. It was followed immediately by a decisive *yes*. I was led into the room where his body lay on a gurney. I was grateful that the sheet was not pulled over his head. That would have been the catalyst to push me over the brink. I remember holding his hand and whispering, "I loved you so much. You were my whole life." *Loved, were*—the enormity and certainty of my loss had already set in.

"Do you want an autopsy performed?" was the next question I had to deal with in my state of shock and detachment. I saw no reason to cut into his body searching for causes. He was dead; an autopsy could not change that. Dead—I was dealing with that word once more. The finality of it riveted through my brain as the question *why* pounded its way to the surface again. *Why* am I here and W. C. is gone? He touched so many lives with love and compassion. He had so much more to give. His zest for living and his enormous energies enabled him to go at a pace that I found impossible. *Why? Why? Why?* I had to find some reason for the disaster that had just engulfed me. But that would have to wait for yet another question. Hospital personnel needed to know which funeral home to call. Without hesitation, I said, "Farris." That settled there was no reason to stay. I knew as we walked away from my beloved husband that he was no longer there—only the body that had housed the soul of that wonderful man for sixty-four years. But it took every bit of courage I had to leave the tangible, touchable, physical personification of the one who had been my life mate for forty-three of them!

The house was filled with people when we returned.

Friends had come to stay with my elderly mother and aunt and to be there for me when I needed them most. Mom was dealing with the same incredulous question. "Oh, honey, this can't be, not W. C.!" she cried. "Why wasn't it me? I'm ninety-three years old; I've lived my life."

I knelt beside her. "I need you, Mom," I said. You're here because I need you so very much. We just don't know the answer to our *whys*."

The process of calling family members and friends was begun. What a terrible message to convey over the telephone. In retrospect, I would have contacted their pastor or a close friend to deliver the message in person to those who would be devastated by the shock.

The campus flag was lowered to half-staff as administrators opened their offices, normally closed on Saturdays, to begin the process of notifying alumni. They searched W. C.'s personnel files in an effort to ferret out the most significant accomplishments for his obituary, which they composed, brought over for approval, and called in to the funeral home.

Friends volunteered to order the casket spray before the florist closed for the weekend. They greeted people at the door, had them sign the register, and visited with them when I could not be present. They manned the telephone and relayed messages. Most of the time I was able to function in a detached sort of way. But there were moments when I needed to be alone to vent my hurt and frustration. I retreated to our room, but I couldn't get away from the reality of my situation. The carpet was still wet where it had been shampooed to remove the blood from W. C.'s head wound. Shoes were strewn about my closet floor from the involuntary jerking of his body. Calamity had come into my life with a swift and savage surge.

"Oh, God," I cried out in desperation. "He was my whole life. I can't live without him." Even as I voiced this anguished plea, I knew, deep down, that I had no other choice!

Our son, Bill, arrived, as did our daughters, Linda and Ann and their families and our foster daughter, Peggy. I was grateful for their presence and for that of other relatives and friends who flocked to my care. Their ministries came at a time when I was unable to function adequately, and freed me to deal with the many decisions related to the immediate needs of the funeral and burial.

Opportunities for such ministering are endless. The bereaved, for instance, is in no state of mind to plan and prepare meals for those who will, of necessity, be there at meal times. Close friends might offer to coordinate efforts for this important function, letting others in the community know what is needed and securing additional refrigeration for excess food. Others may offer to make telephone calls, receive messages or house visiting relatives and friends in their home. Offers to help with the obituary, contact florists, and check with funeral participants will also be appreciated. The key word here is offer. Don't expect the bereaved to ask; in their state of shock, they won't even know what they need.

Though children in the family should not be excluded from the crisis situation, there will be times when grieving adults would welcome your offer to baby sit or to include their children in your family plans. This will take these children from the atmosphere of grief for a little while, but not remove them completely from its reality.

The most important offer of all, however, is the gift of your presence. Be there when the bereaved need to talk. If you are at a loss for words, just listen. Don't try to come up with answers that have eluded generations of learned scholars. None of us really know the answers to the questions they are asking. Let them express whatever emotions they are experiencing without censure on your part. They don't need to feel that certain types of behavior are acceptable and others are not. Reminisce with them, pray with them, cry with them, and, yes, even laugh with them! For through the intense pain an endearing episode that brings a chuckle or two may be remembered, and these snatches of unforgettable nostalgia may lighten the load, at least for the moment.

Reach out and hold the bereaved person's hand. Give them a pat or a comforting hug. Though you cannot really feel the depth of their suffering, you can feel their care. Let them know that you do.

Be there, also, when their house begins to empty as family members return to their own homes and responsibilities. Don't wait for them to initiate that visit. They may not be able to do this for a long time. Help them begin the arduous task of trying to put their lives back together. Gather the dishes and return them throughout the community. Offer to help with the thank you notes. Plan ways to include them in as much activity as they are comfortable with. Look for ways to help. Be aware of their need for privacy, however, and leave when your visit has served its purpose.

A card or a note expressing some of the ways the deceased has touched your life will be treasured. It will also be a source of comfort for a long time, because these are the kinds of communications that are usually kept and referred to again and again. Make a mental note to remember holidays and their special anniversaries during the year, thus keeping them in your care.

I was hardly aware of the maze of activity going on around me as my friends took on my care. Food appeared to feed the multitude of relatives and out-of-town friends who were coming to share our grief and to help make it bearable. It was received and recorded and dishes were labeled. Tables were set, meals served, and cleanup accomplished without my having to give these necessary chores a thought. I was amazed at the response of the College and members of the church and community who provided everything we needed and would later take on the task of hosting a reception for the tremendous number of people attending the funeral.

Truly God works through our network of friends. He provides the love and care we so desperately need and at the same time gives opportunities for nurture to those who long for a way to help. Oh, how grateful I was for this nurture. But through the numbness, through the haze, through the trauma and disbelief, the thought kept returning again and again; this *can't* be happening to me! The fact that my husband had died was indisputable. I *knew* this to be true, but I still couldn't *believe* that it had happened. Shock and denial, the earliest stage of grief, had already engulfed me. It was like a horrible dream—a nightmare—but no amount of denial would allow me to awaken to my neat little world again. This much I knew. This much I could not deny. Reality and denial were waging a diabolical war, and I was the hapless, frightened, uncomprehending victim.

The darkness of night finally descended on my interminable day. I was alone now, alone with my turbulent thoughts, while my family tried to find rest that would help them face the hours ahead. I prayed for oblivion, but the memory of that terrible thud would not go away. The sound of my husband's body crashing to the floor assaulted my ears as the image of my comatose mate rampaged through my tormented mind. The massive heart attack that had claimed his life earlier in the day had changed my world forever.

My heart raced as panic set in. The pain of losing my beloved mate was compounded by the fact that life without him was both inconceivable and terrifying. "Please, God, help me," I prayed. "Give me the strength to go on."

My thoughts continued to churn. A flashback to our wedding found us standing before the altar pledging our vows to each other. This time there were no ominous overtones, no thoughts of impending doom. "Till death us do part," we were saying. But death was a lifetime away and the reference to it simply a promise of the long and wonderful journey we were about to embark upon.

Abruptly the darkness of my soul rejoined the darkness of the night and the stark reality surfaced again. That journey had not lasted a lifetime for both of us. Forty-three years had elapsed and it was now ended.

Tears soaked my pillow as I relived the terrible events of the day—the longest and most horrifying of my entire existence. W. C. was gone. I would never see him again in this life. I didn't even have a chance to say goodbye!

Sleep would not come. We had arranged for the extended family to be housed in college facilities, but they had chosen to occupy sofas and floors at the house. One by one we found ourselves drifting toward the living room. As the first rays of light beckoned the arrival of a new day, that room was filled with wall-to-wall people. Though our family circle had been broken in the most devastating way imaginable, those of us who were left had bonded together to face our grief head on.

The newspaper arrived and another first was ours to experience—checking the obituaries and knowing that we weren't scanning randomly. This time it was real; this time it was ours.

Words from a book I had recently read, *The Greatest of These is Love*, by Charles L. Allen, came to mind with a glimmer of hope. "The psalmist said, 'Yea, though I walk through the valley . . . .' Along the pathway of every life are some valleys. Love underscores the word through. It knows the valley is not the end."[1] Deep in my heart I knew this to be true. And so I greeted the second day of the rest of my life with renewed pleas for strength and with the assurance that my God would not forsake me.

"I am with you and will remain with you always," He promised. Thus, I entered into a partnership with Him and we began our journey through the ups and downs of a turbulent grief experience.

CHAPTER II

CELEBRATING A VICTORIOUS LIFE

"Well done, thou good and faithful servant: . . . enter thou into the joy of thy Lord." (Matthew 25:21)

HILE friends and relatives can, and do, take over many of the tasks that need to be done, there are some things that the immediate members of the family must do for themselves. The visit to the funeral home is one of the hardest. This comes at a time when the bereaved is still numb, which probably makes it easier to deal with decisions that have to be made. Isn't it marvelous that God provides for our needs, even in His grieving process?

Arrangements must be made for cremation or for burial in ground or in a mausoleum, and purchase of a casket and vault or an urn. Time and place of the visitation and funeral are set and limousine needs determined. A list of pallbearers and honorary pallbearers is essential, as are birth and death dates of the deceased. Automatic? Everyone should know these? Of course they should, and would, under ordinary circumstances. But minds can go blank when you are in a state of shock. Try coming up with the full name of the deceased's mother and father when you're not even sure at the precise moment what your own name is.

Then there are decisions about clothing. Will you purchase them from the funeral home or use items from your loved one's own wardrobe? Do you want flowers or would you rather designate a fund to which memorials may be sent?

Consideration must be given to whether you want an open or closed casket, casket spray or pall, memorial service or funeral and/or graveside rites.

Death certificates need to be ordered. A certified copy is required by each bank, credit union, pension plan, insurance company, and the court. Family members traveling on emergency leave also need them for air carriers and places of employment. Ordering enough so that reordering delays will not be a problem is a gigantic task when everything within you resists ordering them at all! These are the things you have to think about at a time when you long to suspend thinking altogether.

I dreaded the visit to the funeral home, but it could not be avoided. The genuine caring and the dignified, courteous manner in which even the minutest detail was taken care of, however, was a tribute to an institution that is probably last on anyone's list of firms they are anxious to do business with.

We did not need to concern ourselves with clothing. W.C. had been scheduled to preach in Chattanooga on Sunday, as he did on many occasions, bringing the mission of our three conference colleges before congregations throughout Holston. He had selected clothing the night before and had everything ready to place in the suitcase prior to our departure. They were sent, instead, to the funeral home.

Our visitation was scheduled for the night before the funeral, though it was with some trepidation that I agreed to this customary experience. I had never been convinced of its validity or, indeed, of its necessity. Am I going to be able to hold up, I wondered; how can I possibly cope? These questions raced through my mind as I faced the dreaded event. "Please help me, God," I pleaded. "I have to do this for W. C."

You're doing it for yourself, too—the thought forged its way to the surface of my consciousness—and for the many other people who are also grieving tonight. Calmness came over me that I could only explain as God's presence. My silent plea to the throngs who were beginning to enter the chapel was—don't be afraid to talk to me, to hold my hand, to embrace me. I might break down, but I won't break. I need to hear how much my husband meant to you. I need to know that you share my loss. I need to grieve with you as you grieve with me.

We had chosen an open casket, perhaps because it was customary, but also because there were many who might wish to look upon his face one more time while they said their good-byes. Often families choose to keep the casket closed so that the deceased may be remembered as a vital, living person. This, as in all funeral arrangements, is a matter of personal choice. There are no "shoulds" or "should nots."

Other decisions that need attention will also come up—decisions about where the continuing influx of out-of-town relatives and friends will be housed, who will ride in the limousine and cars, who will be asked to sit with the elderly, and who, among the many volunteers, will stay at the house during the visitation and funeral. The time for departure needs to be clearly determined so that everyone will be ready to become a part of the funeral procession.

W. C. and I had talked about the need to discuss our own funeral wishes, so that each would know what the other wanted. We had not gotten around to it, however, and I was left with the helpless feeling of not knowing what, but realizing that I wanted something very special for my very special man.

Though crushed by their inexplicable loss, our children were pillars of strength as they helped make funeral arrangements. What comfort it was to have them for support and input! Their father was a beloved personage. His funeral needed to eulogize his life and give testament to his good works. It needed to emphasize his importance as a child of God and his faith in this benevolent God. It also needed to bring the community together to begin the healing process that would enable us to go on without him. We shall always be grateful to our chaplain, the Reverend Hal Hartley, who helped us plan just such a fitting tribute and celebration of W. C.'s life. He worked with the children and me, offering suggestions and finalizing plans. He clarified all aspects of the service, including graveside rites and contents of the printed bulletin. Participants and honorary participants were notified by him and arrangements made for their travel and lodging. He worked with campus security and the funeral home as they provided an escort for the procession and organized parking. He even remembered to have the service taped.

The myriad of details that needed to be dealt with was mind-boggling. I'm sure that I left something undone or forgot to include someone or some group. I hope I have been forgiven for these lapses.

"The funeral is your gift of love," states Doug Manning in his book, *Don't Take My Grief Away*. "Remember, as an act of love you are preparing your memorial to a loved one. Whatever and whoever fits your plans for this memorial is right."[1]

W. C.'s funeral would be an act of love; it was the last thing I could do for him to show that love and I wanted it to be a beautiful celebration of this wonderful life that I had been so proud to share.

We visited the funeral home a few hours before the scheduled service. Tears rolled down my cheeks as I touched W. C.'s hand for the last time. Bittersweet memories flooded back—memories of the many times we had been cautioned on our trip to the Holy Land to stop holding hands in public.

This was my last opportunity. This was my last good-bye. I was glad for the support of our children.

Funerals should be a celebration of the deceased's life. If we truly believe that he has entered into a joyous new relationship with God, why should we view negatively the natural process of death, which is as much a part of life as birth itself? Easier said than done, isn't it, when we are also dealing with a tremendous, life-shattering loss?

The rafters rang as an overflow crowd paid tribute to their beloved professor, colleague, and friend. Ten ministers participated in the memorial to this remarkable man—ten ministers, one college president, and representatives of the faculty, staff, student body, and alumni of Emory & Henry College. For the first time in memory the faculty of the College, dressed in academic regalia, assembled on the campus and marched the half mile or so to the cemetery in solemn procession to pay honor and respect to their colleague. Bishop Clay Lee, our presiding bishop, gave the eulogy, which captured the very heart and spirit of my beloved husband. A message was read from Bishop Earl Hunt, a long-time friend, who was unable to come because of a pressing commitment. As the college choir sang "Going Home," the only request W. C. had ever made concerning his funeral, I could almost visualize the journey his spirit had taken as it wended its way to his eternal home. And I knew, beyond a shadow of a doubt, that as he entered the realm of yet a higher calling, "Well done, thou good and faithful servant," resounded throughout the heavens!

I was glad that the children in our family had been allowed to make their own decision about attending. Doug Manning emphasises the importance of helping children who have varying degrees of understanding deal with their loss. They should be encouraged to express their feelings with the assurance of a non-judgmental listening ear and should be allowed to participate in the funeral process. Even children under two years of age who will not understand death need to be assured of your love, for they, too, will sense that something is wrong.[2]

Our nine year old great-niece came from out of town because she felt she *needed* to be there. She and W. C. had spent many hours discussing theology—theology that she was better able to understand because her uncle had been there for her. One grandson chose not to attend, but changed his mind at the last minute. The others knew from the beginning that they would walk down that aisle with us. The children had also been to the visitation. They realized that W. C. was not sleeping. They knew that he would not return in this life. They saw the manifestations of our grief, and were thus enabled to express theirs in their own way. They also got a glimpse of a life to come—a life that became less threatening because of the uplifting tone of these two events.

A funeral should give this kind of help to those who mourn. It should hold out the promise of eternal life for all who believe. If it also touches on the funny and endearing things that were a part of the person who is no longer with us—something that we can hang on to in the next few weeks and months—we are fortunate. Dr. Charles Sydnor, President of the College, did this for us. In addition to describing at great length W. C.'s absolute passion for a dish of strawberries and ice cream, he ended his remarks with an amusing recollection of his penchant for pronouncing certain words in "Masonese." Through tears our daughter, Linda, whispered, "Moss-a-kins," and I had to smile. That was an "in joke," her dad's unorthodox pronunciation of the word moccasin for as long as either of us could remember.

But the burst of laughter that initiated healing came from the writings of W. C. himself as his amusing response to a faculty recognition award was read. Citing a number of unconventional and hilarious activities engaged in by students through the years, particularly during his role as dean of students, he ended up on a more serious note. "But they are my kind of people, and I pray daily for those here now, for those who have been a part of this great college in the years gone by, and for those in the future who will be fortunate enough to join the student body at Emory & Henry College."

As the faculty processed on foot escorting his body to its final resting place on a hill overlooking the college he loved so much, "For all the saints, who from their labors rest . . ." was still echoing in our thoughts. Rest for this saint, however, would be out of character. In the words of Ms. Lori Saunders, student body president, he was probably at that precise moment "busy reorganizing Heaven and serving on one of God's committees."

We who had gathered to celebrate this victorious life came away with a peace of our own. Though "our sorrows, like sea billows" *did* roll, we could still sing with assurance, "It is well, it is well with my soul!"

"W. C. Mason was our common ground, our vital center, our living reminder of what we and the institution should aspire to be and to achieve."
(Dr. Charles W. Sydnor, former president, Emory & Henry College)
From the engraving of the memorial plaque to Dr. Mason.

CHAPTER III

THE STRUGGLE FOR SURVIVAL

"Be strong and of good courage; be not afraid, neither be thou dismayed: for the Lord thy God is with thee, whithersoever thou goest."
(Joshua 1:9)

OUR days after W. C.'s death representatives from *The Whitetopper*, our campus student newspaper, asked for an interview. I can't, I thought. But I knew that I must. W. C.'s loss had been devastating, not only to his family, but to the entire college community. We were trying to find our way through the shock and the pain. This world, our campus in particular, was a better place because W. C. had passed through, lingered for a while, and given all that he had. We were feeling an emptiness that defies description. Students were walking around in a daze. Colleagues were wondering who to go to for answers. Even the president was lamenting the loss of "the glue" that held his campus together. The beautifully executed issue of the paper was dedicated to the memory of W. C. Little did I realize when I was a reporter for *The Whitetopper* that someday students like me would be preparing such an edition for my husband. It was instrumental in hastening the healing process and enabling the campus to function productively again. I treasure its pages. There had been no doubt in my mind that W. C. was loved. I knew that he had given far beyond anyone's expectations. But I wasn't prepared for the

magnitude and depth of his influence on the world in which he lived.

A week had not yet elapsed; it was too early to deal with dismantling his office, but the children had to go home and I couldn't face doing it without them. We also felt the need of clearing out personal possessions so the new director of religious life could move in as soon as one was employed. Though these kinds of things often have to be done very soon after the death of a loved one, they should be delayed as long as possible. Can the bereaved possibly know how they will feel about the possessions when the numbness wears off? And, can they expect to use good judgment when they are not yet capable of judicious thinking? Major decisions, such as selling the house or moving away, should not be made for at least a year, maybe longer.

I am reminded of a friend who couldn't face going back into her empty home after her husband's death. She put it on the market immediately and moved to another state to be near her daughter. The sale was soon accomplished, but within a few months she realized her mistake. While she enjoyed living close to her family, she found it difficult to adjust to the fact that working parents and teen-aged children couldn't possibly spend as much time with her as she wanted or needed. Unable to make friends as easily in a big city, she sat in her neat little cottage and brooded. If only she could go back to her own home with all its wonderful memories—if only she could find herself again in familiar surroundings, among friends of many years—how happy she would be. But it was too late. She learned, much to her dismay, that it would have been better to delay momentous decisions until she had lived with her grief for a time. Had she done so, she would have avoided the years of additional suffering that this decision added to her grief process.

Once the funeral is over, family and out of town friends begin returning to their homes. I was fortunate that my family members were able to extend their visit. They were there to help us as we attempted to return to normal living. But the loneliness was still oppressive. "Loneliness comes in only one size—Extra Large," said Doug Manning.[1] How true; how utterly, utterly true!

My loss was painful. The person with whom I had shared my innermost thoughts was gone. There was a vacant place in my heart, a vacant place at the table, a vacant place in my bed. I could no longer inch over to W. C.'s side, feel his strong arms encircle me, and fall asleep knowing that all was well with my world. That world had not been free of worries or concerns, to be sure, but as long as we had each other, it had been secure. I had been protected and loved in a relationship that protects and loves like none other. I'd glance longingly at the empty space and pray for strength to face the hours ahead. I couldn't imagine not having W. C. by my side for the rest of my life. I prayed for help in building a meaningful existence without him.

Sleep would finally come, but the next morning I'd awaken with a start, jolted into awareness that W. C. was not there. For a split second I might forget and search for him to share a thought or ask a question.

I tried not to sit around and feel sorry for myself; at times I didn't succeed. I thought of the retirement years I had looked forward to with such yearning and felt cheated. I wasn't naive enough to believe that W. C. would suddenly find great joy in relaxing and doing the "fun things" people are finally able to do when they enter this phase of their lives. His retirement would have been filled with meaningful projects and worthwhile activities, but it also would have involved travel; it would have involved church, community, and college; it would have involved people; it would have involved me! We had even talked about writing some books together. What lost opportunities!

"Oh, God," I cried out in anguish. "Why didn't you just slow him down without stopping him altogether? I depended on him. He was my *whole* life!" He was my whole life—over and over I had uttered these words in complete desperation. I was not able to comprehend that God was not responsible. Neither was I ready to admit that W. C. could not have been, *must* not have been, my whole life—not if I was to survive!

Tears came often, but I didn't try to stop their flow. Neither did I try to hide them. They were a natural and vital part of God's grief process and they brought cleansing and healing. I felt His presence, perhaps more than at any time in my entire life. I never knew when something would spark a memory and open the floodgates. But there was always a shoulder to cry on, a listening ear, and a friend who really cared. I was fortunate, indeed.

The depression and loneliness we experience from a significant loss are overwhelming. They hammer away at us until we can think of nothing else. Nights are the hardest, nights and weekends. Because there is much to do, we are able to function well during the day. Business matters have to be handled, such as applying for pensions, insurance benefits, and social security. The bank must be notified and insurance and investment beneficaries changed. Credit cards need to be reissued in the survivor's name and professional journals cancelled or redirected along with the constant flow of work-related mail. The will must be filed and medical and funeral bills paid. Oh, the mountains of paperwork that these procedures generate and the tremendous amount of time they consume. This is good. They take us away, for a little while, at least, from deep yearning and helpless despair. They give us something to focus on and are instrumental in helping us get through the stage of grief we are in at the time.

Sorting through the deceased's possessions in an effort to make them available to others is traumatic. It is a gigantic task that can't be accomplished all at once. Items that were hardest for us to part with were the "lucky" red socks W. C. had always worn to football games, the Christmas tie that played "Jingle Bells," and the red and green plaid vest and cap that were familiar attire at our family celebrations. They are now a part of someone else's family traditions and are bringing as much laughter and cheer to them as they did to us.

Deciding on a monument is also a major task. We already had the family marker and cornerstones in place. We simply chose for W. C.'s headstone the inscription, "Well Done, Thou Good And Faithful Servant," carved between entwined wedding rings and the United Methodist Clergy symbol. I find it comforting to have my name next to his on the tombstone. I don't even mind my birth date jutting out for all to see. The space beneath it is a reminder that someday there will be a reunion.

I was struggling. I freely admitted to close friends that this was the most devastating experience I had ever encountered. There were times when I felt I couldn't live through it; there were times when I admitted that I didn't want to. What a joyous relief it would have been to join W. C. and continue our journey together. No marriages in Heaven? So be it. But, the God who created life, the God who created birth, the God who created the marvelous, intricate body that we call human, and the God who created the soul that makes us yearn for spiritual fulfillment—that God must have some pretty miraculous surprises for us in the next phase of our existence.

Trusting Him brings assurance that there will be an opportunity for us to be reunited with our loved ones. Death will part us for only a short time. We might never be able to snuggle up in their arms again, but we can have faith that our God will provide a way for His followers to experience warmth and love and belonging. We don't have to know how; we just have to believe that it is so.

Realizing that God still had a purpose for me on this earth, however, I prayed for revelation, for guidance and for strength to follow His leading.

Much of the time I was still walking around in a fog, doing things automatically with no real thought of how or why. You see, even the initial stage of shock, with its numbness and stupor, does return. There is no cause for alarm unless it consumes you totally and makes you unable to function for long periods of time.

I went through the motions of normal routines, but I felt no joy in accomplishment. My house needed cleaning, my garden hoeing, my yard raking, but I couldn't make myself do what had never been unwelcome tasks before. Unable to sleep, I tackled the mounds of paper work covering my desk. I longed to go home, but I *was* home. No, I was in a house that loomed empty without my mate. I had to redefine *home* and give up that which it had formerly meant. If it were to be a safe haven for me again, I would have to accept its new dimensions and strive to keep its warmth and love alive.

Grief has a peculiar way of bringing back the restlessness and longing of our teenage years. The peace and contentment that have been ours for a long time begin to elude us. Our world no longer makes sense. Our loved one will never walk through the door again and cheerfully call our name. There are moments, however, when we feel almost normal again. We think that we are ready to do something we

The Struggle For Survival

haven't been able to muster enough courage for, so we venture out. My first such experience was a trip to the mall. W. C. was a "born shopper." He loved malls and knew the location of hundreds he had become acquainted with through work-related travel. This trip was a big undertaking for me. The sadness was overwhelming, but I was determined. In store after store I encountered W. C.'s favorite shopping niches, always with memories of what he had found enjoyment in buying or what he had browsed through with eager anticipation of coming across a great bargain.

Suddenly my world stopped. I was suspended in time as a familiar looking figure with an engaging smile approached. No, it *can't* be, I wanted to scream. The realization that I would never see W. C. walk down a store aisle again sickened me. My eyes chanced to rest on a sundial with the words, "Grow old with me. The best is yet to be." I panicked. Darting to another department, I regained my composure and dared myself to go on. My faith in a God who sustains me each moment of each day was not shaken. Like the clouds that hide the sun as it struggles to shine through, my gloom could not be penetrated. But there was a stirring deep within that said, "Things will get better; hang on to the hope that you are going to be okay—someday."

This hope stayed with me, even when an unexpected event triggered the depression again. I answered the phone one night and a pleasant voice asked, "Is Dr. Mason there?" I wasn't prepared for this. Didn't *everyone* know that he was dead?

"May I take a message?" I stammered, for loss of a suitable response.

"When will he be home?" the caller persisted.

Oh, God, I thought. I can't say it. But I heard myself answering, "I'm sorry. Dr. Mason died in February."

"Dr. Mason, *Jr!*" she exclaimed.

"Yes," I whispered.

"Well, thank you very much,"—then came the click that terminated the conversation. Most people who had called earlier had expressed sympathy and regret. I realized that the shock was great and a more appropriate answer had eluded the caller, as it had also eluded me.

I still did not understand all of the *whys* of my situation, but they no longer haunted me. I had accepted the fact that it was and that it would always be. Glimpses of hope were now shining through the depression, shock, and pain. No wonder grief is such a bewildering experience.

"Grief is as much about finding as it is about losing," according to Bob Deits in *Life After Loss*. "It is not a social disease, but a process of recovering your balance after life has dealt you a major blow. There is one decision confronting you that dominates all others at this point in time: You must choose to live again."[2]

And we must—we simply must make that choice! Though the struggle for survival will go on, we can be secure in the knowledge that there is hope for tomorrow. Our task is to use the talents God had given us, to live up to our potential, to make a life for ourselves that will be vastly different from anything we have ever known. And, in the process, we must believe that it can and will be rewarding.

CHAPTER IV

FRANTIC ACTIVITY OR PURPOSEFUL ENDEAVOR?

"Be still, and know that I am God: . . ."
(Psalm 46:10)

DID everything I could think of to stay busy. I had to be doing something every waking moment. I walked, I swam, I scrubbed floors, I even washed windows. I began revising old manuscripts and sending them on their journey to prospective publishers. I spent hour upon hour writing W. C.'s memoir for the Conference Journal. I visited his office and took gifts to his administrative assistant and his work-study students. I even gave a big Easter Egg Hunt for community children. Filling my days with exhausting activity kept me too occupied to think constantly about my loss, but it didn't erase the memories that crowded into my sleepless nights. And so I filled them also. I worked into the morning hours, trying to stay so busy that when I finally fell into bed I'd be exhausted enough to sleep. It didn't help. I was completely drained, but my mind continued on with a relentlessness that refused to give up. I'd cry into my pillow until the wee hours of the morning when my fatigued brain would finally give in to my bone-tired body and allow it the rest it craved. Sometimes I'd get desperate enough to will my mind to cease functioning. With a fierce determination I'd repeat over and over again, "Sleep, sleep, sleep," as I pushed all thoughts from the surface before they had time to entrench themselves in my consciousness. I'd awaken the next

morning with a vivid recollection of that monotonous repetition and a feeling of accomplishment as I realized that God was with me, indeed, but He expected some effort on my part. This grief process was a journey *with* Him, not by Him.

I invited people for meals and took Mom and Ethel out for dinner, but I couldn't eat. Food stuck in my throat. Sixty pounds melted from my grateful body along with most of my rheumatic aches and pains. I liked the change and resolved not to regain the weight. So much for resolutions.

Weight lost during a grief experience is almost always regained. We can count on it. Sometimes we go from being unable to swallow food to shoveling it in without even tasting it, not because we are hungry, but because food has become a crutch. We eat when we are lonely or upset. We may not recognize this behavior for what it is, but we must, if we are to control it.

Other physical symptoms may begin to crop up—headaches, shortness of breath, all kinds of pains. They are not imaginary. I was having lunch with friends one day when an excruciating pain shot through my right ankle making it impossible to walk. Thinking that the surgical pin holding an old compound fracture together or the steel reconstruction of the socket had torn loose, they took me to the specialist who had cared for the injury years earlier. X-rays revealed "all artillery intact." The completely unbelievable diagnosis was gout.

"Surely you don't expect me to go out there and tell my friends I have gout!" I exclaimed.

He laughed. "I have it myself and it's not *always* caused by drinking and high living," he retorted. That was consolation, of sorts, but I still had to deal with the fact that I would be laid up and my elderly mother and aunt would have to assume my care. The husband to whom I had always gone for solace was no longer there. "Please help me, God," I whispered. "I can't help myself and I am so frightened."

Perhaps my body was reacting to the raised level of uric acid brought on by stress. Perhaps it was telling me to slow down. I don't know, but being off of my feet for a while gave me an opportunity to make a sizeable crater in the stack of thank you notes that had only been dented. My children had offered to assist me or to write them for me, but I wanted to do it myself. It took many months, but I finally corresponded with all who had reached out to me in love and concern.

Writing these notes was therapeutic. If offered me the opportunity to relive precious moments with those who had respected and loved my husband. It also gave me a chance to read again their expressions of concern at a time when I could comprehend them better and etch them into my memory. I keep the cards and letters in a basket in W. C.'s study. From time to time I browse through them and am reminded of God's goodness and His remarkable perception in endowing His creatures with emotions such as empathy, compassion, and love.

With my forced slowdown I realized that frantic endeavor in an effort to blot out the pain was not helpful. Neither was it productive. The activities that had kept me in a frenzy were all worthwhile, but I was doing them for the wrong reasons. I was taxing myself beyond my limits of endurance in an effort to run away from my pain. Staying busy was helpful, but bustling around to the point of exhaustion was not. Filling the emptiness with selective pursuits within the confines of my physical and emotional strength was the next task I needed to tackle.

I opened the Bible one day and the words of Psalm 46:10 jumped out at me. "Be still and know that I am God . . .." Be still, I thought; I haven't been still for such a long time. I closed my eyes and let God's peace flow over me. With it came the realization that I couldn't run away. I had to allow myself to feel the loneliness and sadness. I had to cry those tears. They were vital aspects of the healing process.

Another day's meditation led me to 1 Corinthians 3:16, "Know ye not that ye are the temple of God and that the Spirit of God dwelleth in you?" I didn't need a loud, thundering voice to convince me that this was a direct message from God.

"Forgive me, God," I beseeched, "and help me do all that is within my power to make Your temple whole again, not only physically, but spiritually and emotionally as well. I know that You have a purpose for me. Please give my life direction."

Reading *Up From Grief*, by Bernadine Kreis and Alice Pattie helped me focus on where I was in the grief process, and where I needed to go. "To help yourself takes time and the courage to face the truth without flinching. Little use to pick up the pieces of what you were and try to patch them together. What you were is history. Yesterday is over; let it linger, for it will anyway, to enhance and deepen the dimensions of your character—but concentrate on today."[1] Concentrate on today, I thought. Of course, that is what I must do. Yesterday is gone, irretrievably, and tomorrow too painful to think about. But today I can deal with. At least I can try.

I had already accepted that which I could not change. The thrust of my living now needed to be directed toward making whatever changes *were* possible and only God could provide me with the courage and the ability to do that.

Chapter 10 of *When Life Is the Pits*, by Robert Reccord, is entitled *Moving in the Flow of God's Will*. The title intrigued me and I read this chapter a number of times in order to digest its message. But how can we know, beyond a shadow of doubt, what God's will is for us, I pondered. And then one sentence stood out above the others. "One of the key principles of life is that in order to know what God desires to do with your life requires a commitment to God of your life."[2] Just twenty-nine words, but oh, the impact they have. Once we have committed our life to Him, with no reservations, we will have little trouble discerning His will for us.

My prayer for purpose and direction was soon answered. As my body mended, the despair began to be replaced with hope and determination. I thought about the stories I had written based on experiences in the life of each of my grandchildren. They had a message I wanted to impart. Dialogue and action that might bring them up to publishing standards began popping into my head and I found myself engrossed in the revision process. I was doing something that I enjoyed. I was doing something that I felt was worthwhile and I was concentrating on something other than my loss. I was expending energy, yes, but I was no longer running away. I had accepted my physical limitations and had paced my activities accordingly. I felt, truly felt, that I was beginning to "move in the flow of God's will." Frantic activity was finally being replaced with purposeful endeavor and the physical symptoms of distress vanished.

W. C. WITH HIS FATHER, CLIFFORD

W. C. WITH HIS MOTHER, MYRTLE AND HIS BROTHER, GLENN

CHAPTER V

YEARNING FOR THE PAST

"The Lord is my strength and my shield; my heart trusted in him, and I am helped: therefore my heart greatly rejoiceth; and with my song I will praise him."
(Psalm 28:7)

EARNING for the past sometimes makes us go to the opposite extremes of frantic endeavor. Instead of filling our lives with frenzied activity in an effort to run away from our pain, we fall into the trap of sitting around and dreaming about the past, yearning for its return and doing nothing to move ourselves into accepting our new situations and reentering life. This is an invitation for depression. Be aware of the danger if you find yourself responding to grief for long periods of time in this manner. If you are not ready to return to a former interest, find something new. Your feelings of self-worth are at stake.

If we don't want to spend the rest of our lives in a diminished state, we must choose to jolt ourselves out of the doldrums. Friends can help, but we have to accept their offers. We may even have to take the first step, and the next, and the next. Force yourself to concentrate on the positive. Seize every opportunity that comes your way for purposeful and rewarding ventures, being careful not to swing the pendulum of activity into a frenzied state. Look for ways to help others. Take up a hobby. Go back to work. Find some group whose emphasis grabs your attention and volunteer.

Become involved in life again, at least on a short-term basis. It needn't be total involvement at first, but as you break out of yesterday's mold you are freeing yourself to fashion new patterns. As you knead and sculpt these different traits that are beginning to characterize a "new you", a way of life that holds great promise for the future could be emerging.

"The order and speed at which each person travels through grief is individualized to his or her own needs," according to Elizabeth Brown, author of *Sunrise Tomorrow*. "The most difficult stage to traverse and pass is the yearning stage. Release comes when you let go of the yearning for life to be what it was before the death."[1]

Though Elizabeth Brown was speaking about the death of their young daughter, the intense yearning for life to be what it had been was one with which I, too, was wrestling. Unable to let go of that yearning, life for me continued to vacillate between the various stages of grief. Because of the suddenness of W. C.'s death, there had been little time for bargaining. Denial had lasted only a short while, for the reality that this not only could happen, but that it had happened surfaced with deadly force during the first few hours. Depression and its sadness had taken over, interspersed with occasional glimpses of partial acceptance and hope. I was making progress, but hurdles kept springing up in my path.

Three months had elasped and graduation was upon us. "I can't attend, God," I confessed. "A graduation without W.C.?—unthinkable!" I willed time to stand still, but it forged ahead with accelerating speed. I pushed thoughts of the dreaded occasion from my mind, but they bounced back with unrelenting force. Oh, how I yearned for things to be *normal* again. I wanted my husband. I wanted my marriage. These yearnings tore at my very core, but they didn't return my neat little world tied up in a ribbon-adorned package. I thought about staying away from the commencement activities, but I couldn't do that either. I prayed for strength to face these events that I knew would be traumatic. I was invited to all the festivities, partly because I had been invited in the past, partly because I was still considered "family," and certainly because posthumous awards were being presented to my wonderful husband. I couldn't let the College down; neither could I fail to be on hand to accept the gracious outpouring of love and respect from W. C.'s students, alumni, and peers.

The College had done everything possible to help us through this period of grieving and to ensure that W. C. would be remembered forever for the vital role he had played in its recent history. His duties had been redistributed, new faculty hired, and outside organizations recruited to continue some of his programs. The Board of Governors of Emory & Henry College and the Trustees of Holston Conference Colleges passed a resolution naming the offices and fellowship hall of Memorial chapel in his memory. Awards by the student body, in addition to the memorial issue of *The Whitetopper*, were the dedication of their 1990 yearbook to his memory and presentation of their Excellence in Teaching award to me on his behalf. An endowed scholarship was also established in his name by his many friends and co-workers. Resolutions from organizations throughout the area filled my scrapbook, as did articles written in newspapers and magazines, all attesting to his enormous capacity to make a difference in the lives of those he touched. What an outpouring of respect and love!

Perhaps he would have been embarrassed at the many accolades accorded him, but deep down, I think he would have also been thrilled. I could visualize the smile forming at the corners of his mouth, spreading across his face, and breaking into that famous grin.

And so I went to graduation. I suppose wild horses couldn't have kept me away. I wasn't prepared, however, for the effect the faculty procession would have on me. Since I couldn't turn and run, I stood there and watched W. C.'s replacement as faculty marshal direct the proceedings. For the first time since his death I realized that the college not only could, but was, going on without him. Surely there must be a lesson somewhere in all of this for me.

The ceremony was finally over and we went home. Oh, how I had looked forward to this moment in years past. After a fevered pace of frantic activity that culminated in this beautiful and meaningful event, W. C. could finally relax and we would spend the rest of the day, even the rest of the weekend together. Indeed, commencement each year signaled a somewhat more relaxed schedule for the next few months and I treasured it dearly. Now I was facing it with dread and I realized that this event would probably always bring nostalgia.

One other milestone remained, Annual Conference. We usually arrived on Sunday, a day before the sessions began. This gave us time to relax, to settle in and enjoy the peace and tranquility of Lake Junaluska before the four-day frenzy of conference activities descended upon it.

I awakened with a heavy heart on the day we would have been starting out, eager to be with our friends and take part in this yearly adventure that had become an important part of our lives. Would W. C. know conference was going on without him? Did he know about the sick feeling in the pit of my stomach, the wretched, breath-taking sobs that wanted to escape and would before the day was over? I wondered who would assemble the Emory & Henry display. He had done it for years.

I went to church and felt God's calming presence, walked to the cemetery, sat on the bench by W. C.'s grave, and let the tears flow. Totally exhausted, I was ready to accept the comfort and solace that had been hovering over me all day. The presence of God in my life was real.

A few days later we made the trip to Junaluska. I had agreed to stand with one of W. C.'s students as he was being ordained and our family was to be in attendance at the memorial service. For the last few years I had come to that service wondering how I would ever be able to attend when it was my turn to sit in the family section. It was a comfort to have Mrs. Hunt, President Sydnor and Chaplain and Mrs. Hartley with us. Bishop Hunt delivered the memorial address. I was grateful for his marvelous message.

The hustle and bustle of Conference business had been underway for several days before we arrived. I missed being a part of the non-stop "kitchen cabinet" sessions. No longer a participant, I seemed to be standing on the outside looking in. Sharing W. C.'s life and ministry had been a rare privilege, but this era of my life was now over. I missed being his wife; I missed being a minister's wife; I missed being married. I had not only lost my husband; I had lost my role in life. Yearning for the past was overwhelming, but the aspects of that past I wanted so desperately to recapture could never again be a part of my experience. Resolving to put behind me that which was already gone, I redoubled my efforts to face a world that no longer included W. C.

I prayed for strength to live one day, one hour, even one moment at a time. The knowledge that he would never return was there, but the oppressive, earth-shattering pain that had once wracked my whole being with unrelenting savageness was gone. In its place was a dull ache, a steady throb that accompanied every breath and became as automatic as breathing itself. Would it ever go away, I wondered. Would I ever feel joy as well as sorrow?

Even as I asked myself these questions, the answers were forming in my mind. Yes, I affirmed. The assurance that I would survive was beginning to surface.

At home again I accepted all invitations to be with those who included me in their plans. I initiated get-togethers with friends. I focused my energies on achieving satisfaction through avenues that were available to me.

My world had not been safe for more than four months. It was time for me to put stability back into it, to start assuming responsibility for this new phase of my life. Though my aunt had moved back to Florida, Mom was still with me and I wanted to make a loving and stable home for her.

I dreaded early mornings and late evenings. Most of all, I dreaded Sundays. But God had granted my petitions. There were fewer tears and moments of utter devastation. I honestly felt that I was making progress, but it was not without its setbacks.

Participation in a church school discussion group using Maxie Dunnam's book, *Living The Psalms*, was therapeutic. We were asked to recall our earliest recollection of hearing the Twenty-Third Psalm and to reflect upon the occasion when this psalm was most meaningful. I couldn't come up with a precise memory of the first time I had heard this marvelous passage. It seemed that it had always been there for me. I did remember, however, learning to recite it along with other memory verses. I was probably twelve years old at the time.

I didn't have to search for the times the Twenty-Third Psalm had been most meaningful. It had been a source of great strength and comfort on at least three occasions—each of which represented traumatic events in my life. All involved grief. The first was when W. C. and I had read it together after the miscarriage that ended our second pregnancy and shattered our dreams. The next time that stood out in my memory was when W. C. held my hand and read it to me just before I went into life-threatening surgery. The third time, I whispered it over and over again in an effort to bolster my strength and courage after W. C.'s death. And now, I was coming to the place in the grief proceess where I could affirm with Dr. Dunnam, "Glory! The Lord is my shepherd."[2] He has been with me through this journey; He will continue to go with me, and I have faith that I will dwell in His house forever.

Harold Kushner's words from *Who Needs God*, came to mind as I further reflected on this Psalm, "God will not bring back your loved one, but he can do the next best thing. He can take you by the hand and guide you through the valley of the shadow of death until you come out again into the sunlight on the other side."[3]

Of course, God would do that for me. I had known that from the beginning, but the fluctuating nature of grief had, from time to time, snatched that assurance from me. Yearnings would continue to come and go, but they would not incapacitate me and I would be able to move through them with relative ease.

"Expect a positive outcome. Anticipate it. Plan for it. It will come," said Colgrove, Bloomfield and McWilliams in their book, *How to Survive The Loss Of A Love*.[4] With fierce determination I proclaimed to myself, for I was the one who desperately needed to hear it—"I will not be a victim. I will move toward eliminating the yearnings. I will expect a positive outcome. I will come out into the sunlight again."

HOLSTON CONFERENCE AND EMORY & HENRY ASSOCIATES
REV. CHARLES NEAL, DR. F. HEISSE JOHNSON,
BISHOP H. ELLIS FINGER, DR. THOMAS
F. CHILCOTE, W. C.

EMORY & HENRY ASSOCIATES
DEAN RICHARD PFAU, PRESIDENT CHARLES SYDNOR,
CHAPLAIN HAL HARTLEY, W. C.

CHAPTER VI

ENABLING SUPPORT, ENABLING LOVE.

"But now abideth faith, hope, love, these three;
and the greatest of these is love."
(1 Corinthians 13:13), ASV.

IVE months into my grief process I was thumbing through a magazine and came upon a psychological test that purported to help one discover one's deep-seated needs. Out of curiosity, I sat down and answered the questions. Then I tabulated and wrote out the assessment of my situation as dictated by my answers. I was amazed. My profile indicated that for me love was what made my world function, but it wasn't functioning as it should. I was missing the security of romantic love such as that found in marriage. It also indicated that I didn't feel safe—that I might be afraid of losing my job or my spouse. My need for affirmation, however, was apparently being met. Wow! I became a believer in those questionnaires, "Johnny on the spot."

No matter how much I wished it were not so, I knew that I was no longer the most important person in the world to another human being. In time that could come, but somehow I didn't imagine that it would. Though I would not rule out the possibility, I didn't really want to develop another romantic relationship. I had already had the best. So I acknowledged to myself that romance was probably not in my immediate future—not in my extended future, not in my future at all—and I was comfortable with that realization.

The fact that my need for affirmation was being met was largely due, I believed, to my family and to the many friends who had showered me with love and concern. The children called often and took turns coming home. Students remained a vital part of my existence. They helped me go on when the going was almost too rough. They took me under their wings—raked the yard, cleaned the gutters and painted the swings. They visited often, telephoned, sent cards and notes and greeted me with hugs whenever we met. They even asked to come over in groups again. Together we weathered the storm of losing an irreplaceable force in our lives. Mom and I enjoyed having them in our home and were grateful that they still wanted to come.

Close friends continued to call and visit. They planned outings and saw that we were included. I knew that God was beside me, not only giving me courage with His presence, but also helping me through the very difficult times via these friends who had bombarded Him with petitions on my behalf and who had kept us constantly in their prayers and in their care. How do people survive grief experiences without this kind of enabling support and love?

Robert Veninga, author of *A Gift of Hope*, says, "Friendships have an immense power to heal a broken spirit. Why? Because we know that our best friends would never walk out on us, no matter how difficult the crisis might be. When a heartbreak occurs, most people are surprised by how many friends they actually have."[1]

I wasn't really surprised, but I was gratified. Not only were they there because it was the thing to do. They were there because they wanted to be there and they continued to be available for the same reason. Never once did I hear, "It's time to put all of that behind you." Never once was I told how to grieve "appropriately." Never once was there even a suggestion that things would be better for me if I did something differently or if I stopped a particular behavior. My friends provided a sounding board for me. They listened when I needed to talk. They didn't offer advice I wasn't ready to accept. They were just there, and I knew it.

Having friends that we can call on is great, but we shouldn't cling to them. They have lives of their own with demands on their time and energy that have nothing to do with us. We cannot allow ourselves to need them all of the time. That would be an easy situation to fall into, but it wouldn't be good for us, or fair to them. We must muster the discipline and courage to create a life of our own that will include, but not burden, those who have reached out to us.

I was fortunate to have two clergy benefactors who were there for me from the beginning. Bishop Hunt called often to remind me of his concern and to give me an opportunity to talk about things that were on my mind. Chaplain Hartley was my "on the scene" mentor, helping me come to grips with the reality of my new world. They provided strength and enabling support as I searched the Scriptures and sought guidance from my mentor above.

It had taken W. C.'s death for me to realize the depth of love that is possible in other aspects of the human experience. It wasn't until I stood in dire need of warmth and affection to help replace that which I had lost that I was able to sense and respond to the magnitude of unconditional love in the lives of family and friends. I became acutely aware of my feelings for others and my deep affection and appreciation for those who had surrounded me with enabling love. This love had brought me through the blind groping, the deep hurt and the stark reality of my new world. I had experienced so much warmth; I simply had to respond in like manner. My reserve vanished as I became more outward in this response. I had always been reluctant to initiate such expressions, but they were beginning to be easy for me. I was becoming a different person. In death, even more than in life, W. C. had helped me understand the most important force in the universe.

I had counted on my effervescent husband to extend the hand of fellowship, to greet people with enthusiasm. I was the "behind the scenes" person who felt very comfortable standing in the background. I had to make my own way now, and because I had no other choice, I became more outgoing. I began paying attention to names, letting them travel up rather than going in one ear and out the other.

The dedication of the fellowship hall and the offices in the chapel to W. C.'s memory was approaching. I was filled with gratitude and pride. The chapel had been his "baby" from the time he climbed the steeple to install the cross until the day he died. I greeted the warm October day and the wonderful service with a grateful heart, then returned home to prepare a reception for Bishop and Mrs. Hunt. My moments of jubilation were muted as I walked past W. C.'s desk and noticed his lucky coin. What kind of luck did it bring him, I thought. He's dead. What does it mean to be dead? How does it feel? Where is Heaven? Is he with loved ones today? He'd rather be with me! Oh, how he'd relish entertaining folks who are coming to our home to visit with the Hunts. And the dedication of the fellowship hall to his memory—why did he have to miss that? What a thrill it would have given him! I allowed myself these thoughts. I allowed myself the luxury of tears. And then I set about readying the house for my guests. I wouldn't be able to greet them with W. C.'s gusto—a warm handshake, a slap on the back, a broad grin. But I could, and I would, greet them with my own more subdued welcome.

I climbed into bed that night and prayed, "Thank you, God, for this wonderful day. Once again, W. C. has been memorialized in such a meaningful way. And once again You have provided me with enabling support and with enabling love."

W. C. would have been proud to know this honor was being bestowed upon him, I thought. Oh, how I wish he could have been there to experience the expressions of love and gratitude by his students, alumni and peers. And then I whispered with satisfaction, "What makes you think he wasn't, old girl?"

I awakened the next morning refreshed from a restful night, probably my first since W. C.'s death. Deep down I knew that there were more stormy days ahead, that I wouldn't always feel this peace, but for the moment it signified hope. God has not promised us a trouble free existence, but He has promised us the stamina and the courage to build from the ashes of our disappointments, bringing order out of chaos and fulfillment out of desolation.

Grief was so hard to live with. Not even I understood my various responses to my life-altering situation. So, I stopped trying to rationalize. Rather than being concerned about what was normal, I tried to dwell on what was healthy. I knew that I had to face grief in my own individual way and that I was going to have the strength to get through it and emerge on the other side intact. I could look ahead and glimpse that outcome for myself because I had a family and a community of friends who had reached out to me in love—the kind of love that is enabling!

I am reminded of a plaque that hung on the kitchen wall of our Damascus Head Start Center. It caught my attention each time I visited my friend and co-worker in her little domain. "Ain't nothing going to happen today that me and the

Lord together can't handle," it read. I had kept that thought ever before me and had called on the Lord to help me through the times when my strength and resolve had not been sufficient to carry my share of the load. I had felt His presence as I struggled to find new meaning and purpose for my life.

"How many times, Lord, have you sent a comforter? And how many times did that comforter supply the enabling support that pushed me into the next step on this journey toward recovery?"

Suddenly, almost as if I had never heard of it, I thought of the Trinity—God, the Father, much as an earthly parent suffering with us and giving us room to grow—God, the Son, undergoing the indignity, the pain, the humiliation of the cross so that we might have redemption from sin—God, the Holy Spirit, filling our very being with His presence and helping us triumph over our struggles and find peace. Here was the supreme example of enabling support and enabling love.

CHAPTER VII

The Fears, The Doubts, The Frustrations

"I sought the Lord, and he heard me, and delivered
me from all my fears."
(Psalm 34:4)

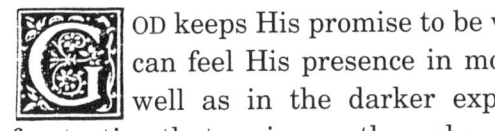OD keeps His promise to be with us in our need. We can feel His presence in moments of assurance as well as in the darker experiences of doubt and frustration that spring up throughout our healing process.

He was there for me as daily events brought renewed awareness of how dependent I had become on W. C. It was difficult now to stand on my own feet. But I couldn't fall apart. That would be letting him down; more important, it would be letting me down. In my frustration I tried to reach out to him, but I felt only emptiness. "I miss you so much," I whispered. "I don't feel like being strong anymore. I want you to hold me, to tell me again how proud you are of me and how much you love me. There are people in my present world who truly care about me, who even love me, and I am grateful. But only you can fill the emptiness that I am feeling today."

I closed my eyes and tried to experience W. C.'s presence. There was no embrace, no soft voice whispering words I longed to hear, no closeness or feeling of companionship. W.C. was gone and I didn't know how to find him. Neither did I know how to carry on without him. Even the routine tasks of running the home seemed impossible.

Though I was familiar with our financial situation, having taken over responsibility for the household budget during our marriage, I was in "left field" when it came to making monetary decisions that would affect my future in such an absolute way. I had not counted on having to do this without my partner.

Dr. Joyce Brothers, author of *Widowed*, states "All married women should prepare themselves financially to be widows, no matter how old they are or how well off their husbands may be. Every married woman should ask herself, 'If my husband were to die tomorrow, what would I have to live on?'"[1] This was probably not as much a concern for me as it might be for younger women who have the responsibility of rearing and educating children. But it was a concern. I was fortunate to have resource persons in each of our financial institutions that provided valuable guidance. I learned to ask for help and accept it gratefully, but I was still apprehensive.

I'd sit at my desk for hours trying to assimilate all I needed to know about pensions, investments, budgets, and income tax. I was afraid. I didn't trust my own judgment on matters of such importance.

Tax time was approaching and W. C. had always prepared the forms. His brother, Glenn, did this for me immediately following W. C.'s death, but I couldn't ask him to do it year after year.

My spirit had been impoverished by my husband's absence, my confidence in my ability to handle financial matters badly shaken. Financial security depended upon my ability to make wise investments, and I didn't know where to start. I felt inadequate, not only in financial matters, but in most day-to-day situations that arose. Why, I didn't even know how to put gas in the car.

The Fears, The Doubts, The Frustrations

The final blow came when I discovered one day that the foundation of my house was crumbling. I stood there in disbelief as my spirits crumbled too. "What else God?" I cried out in dismay and ran to find Mom. I had to get away, if only for a little while. We got into the car and headed toward the mountains. My incredible mother, who seldom let life's tragedies get her down, was able to soothe my spirits as we drove through the beautiful countryside. But a glance at the gas gauge brought renewed panic. It was on empty.

"Please, God," I silently implored, "we need a gas station—now! Mom can't go with me to find help and her angina attacks are coming too frequently to leave her alone." Within minutes I saw a garage and chugged up to its only pump. My spirits hit bottom again; it was self-service. "Read the directions," came the gentle prompting that could only have come from God. I studied them and they seemed fairly simple. I reached for the nozzle, thrust it into the tank, and squeezed the lever. The joy I felt as that pump sprang to life clicking pennies into dollars was exhilarating.

With a sense of gratitude and accomplishment I whispered, "Thank you, God, for answering my prayer—Your way." His care was abundantly clear. He had helped me conquer my fear through this hands-on experience. In the days to come He would show me that knowledge could accomplish the same goal. A financial management course and an estate-planning seminar were being offered in our area. I enrolled reluctantly. Six weeks of classes didn't make me an expert, but they helped me become comfortable with fiscal matters. They also gave me the courage to talk with my banker who steered me through the process of applying for a loan to repair my house. Much to my surprise, I found myself at ease in her office as I negotiated that loan.

Whether I wanted to or not, I had become the head of the household and I had to assume the responsibilities that entailed. Confidence was beginning to replace the panic that had confronted me as the unknown was thrust into my lap.

I found I could do things I didn't dream I was capable of doing. Sometimes I failed, however, and sometimes I decided that the task simply wasn't worth the effort. I could care for that chore in another way. I confronted my fears, my dislikes and the things I found myself putting off. I took my car through a car wash, continued to pump my own gas, and made arrangements for maintenance service. I engaged an income tax consultant. I made major decisions about repairs to the house, removal of trees and installation of a new sewer system.

I began to take control of my life and to feel a sense of accomplishment when I succeeded. My self-esteem took a giant leap. I was functioning autonomously.

There were still days when I felt washed out, tired, unable to get involved in anything. So, I'd have a day in which I wouldn't push myself to accomplish. If I didn't feel like making the bed, I'd close the bedroom door. If I didn't feel like cooking, we'd have soup and sandwiches. These days didn't happen often, but when they did they were accepted without the slightest consternation.

But there were some things that had to be done; the county sticker had expired on my car. I had waited until the last minute to put it on and I couldn't budge the old one. I fussed and fumed and shed a few frustrated tears. Then I remembered the story of *The Little Engine That Could*, by Watty Piper. It had been a favorite in my kindergarten classrooms. The children loved acting it out. I thought about the beaming human engine and ten or so little "earthling" freight cars scampering joyously across the terrain as they found that they could, indeed, get over that imaginary mountain. It brought a smile and a determination to scrape a little harder. As the dull edge of the razor dug into my fingers, the sharp edge slid beneath that decal and peeled it away. Next year I won't wait until the last day. I'll find my scraper or buy a new one. Better yet, I'll get someone to put the decal on for me! I was grateful to the little engine for reminding me that with a little extra effort and a whole lot of faith, *I could*, also!

"Of course you can," my new found boldness cheered me on. "You've never lacked self-confidence to the degree that you are experiencing it now." This was true. In addition to being a helpmate to my minister husband and a mother to my children, I had enjoyed a career in early childhood education and engaged in volunteer activities that involved leadership. Why, then, was I allowing these negative feelings to take over?

My self-induced pep talk continued. "It's time to assert your independence, to put aside the fears, the doubts and the frustrations—to live your life to the fullest, even if that means taking on tasks you'd rather not embrace."

Grief makes a curious impact on our lives. In spite of ourselves, we experience personal growth. Elizabeth Kübler-Ross in her book, *Death—The Final Stages of Growth*, had this to say: "When you fully understand that each day you awaken could be the last you have, you take the time that day to grow, to become more of who you really are, to reach out to other human beings."[2] Each day we awaken is also a gift from God. It behooves us to use it wisely and to follow Ms. Kübler-Ross' admonition to reach out to others and to grow.

Turning to my fellow traveler on this journey of acceptance and faith I declared with conviction, "With Your help,

God, I will try to use my days wisely. With Your help I know that I can do anything." That doesn't mean that I will do things because others think I should. I have to be true to myself, to do those things I feel God is calling me to do, knowing that He will provide the strength and the ability to accomplish tasks that are part of our agenda.

The fears, the doubts, the frustrations—they haven't been completely conquered, not yet. But determination is helping to relegate them to the background. The grief process takes effort, perseverance and persistence. *And* it takes time.

W. C. WITH THE COUPLE HE ALWAYS INTRODUCED AS
"MY FAVORITE MOTHER AND FATHER-IN-LAW,
LAURA AND LEE FREDERICK."

CHAPTER VIII

The Anger, The Guilt, The "What-Ifs"

"Commit thy works unto the Lord, and thy
thoughts shall be established."
(Proverbs 16:3)

HE question of anger began coming up in conversations with some of my friends. Knowing about the stages of grief, they seemed concerned that I might be suppressing this vital emotion. I knew about the stages of grief, also, but I thought I had by-passed this one. I assured them that I was not suppressing anger, that I simply didn't feel it. I explained that I was hurt that the person I loved more than life itself was gone, along with my dreams for retirement years with him and my safe little world. I was frustrated that W. C.'s life had been cut short when he was giving so much and had so much more to give. I further explained that I didn't feel anger because I knew he would have changed if he had understood what he was doing to himself. He thought he could go on forever meeting every need he confronted. Something within him made him strive to do just that and I was grateful that he had made a difference in the lives of so many people. All of these statements were true at that point in time. All of them continued to be true except the denial of anger.

I was making progress, but the reality that I lived with every moment of every day was that my husband would never be there for me again. *Always* had become *our song* early in courtship. In recent years it had not been heard with frequency, but when its soft strains had pealed out over the air waves there was immediate recognition, followed by some acknowledgement of our promise to be there for each other—"not for just an hour, not for just a day, not for just a year—but always."

I was washing dishes one morning, completely oblivious to the chatter coming from the radio. Shocked into reality by the hauntingly familiar, "I'll be loving you, always," I reeled around and tried to flip the switch that would blot out the lyrics I couldn't bear to hear. But my fingers seemed powerless. I stood there and listened. Days had not been fair for me and W. C. hadn't kept his promise! Sobs wracked my body as tears stained my cheeks. I felt the pain in its entire terrifying enormity.

"Why, dear God, why has life dealt me this terrible blow?" I cried. The anger had finally surfaced. I was angry with W. C. for working so hard and leaving me before we could share our golden years. I was angry with God for taking such a dedicated servant when he had so much more to give. I was angry at the world for daring to go on without my wonderful husband.

I grabbed my tools and headed for the cemetery. Thrusting the mattock into rocklike sod that had refused to yield to its onslaught only days earlier, I went about preparing the ground for flowers. I could have dug to China—almost did—and within minutes those flowers were planted. I plopped down on the ground, exhausted. I knew that this anger could not be by-passed if healing was to come about. But I also knew that I needed help.

"My courage is gone, God," I sobbed. "I've tried so hard to get through these months. Just when I think I'm going to succeed, I lose control. I'm floundering; I don't know how to help myself. Please renew my courage. Help me to conquer this anger."

I looked out over the rolling hillside, then into the blue-gray sky. Peace seemed to envelop me as the words of a hymn I had all but forgotten coursed through my mind. "Cast your burdens on the Lord, and leave them there." And leave them there—that was the crucial phrase. I had done a lot of casting during the past seven months, but I had not been able to leave my problems with the Lord. I vowed to do better. The responsibility was on my shoulders. I couldn't just turn the problem over to God and then sit back and expect Him to bring it to a successful conclusion. This was not His journey; it was ours. But I could turn the anger over to Him, thus freeing myself to do the things that would set the healing process in motion.

"Thank you, God, for helping me through this anger," I prayed, "and please forgive me for the hostile thoughts that have ravaged my soul today." Though my ears heard nothing, God's soothing presence had already filled my heart. I knew that I had a right to my anger—I had a right to experience it, vent it, examine it—and then I had a mandate to let it go. God was not shocked; He was suffering through that anger with me and was ready to take it upon Himself, both then and in the days that would follow, for this would probably not be my last outburst of rage.

I gathered my tools and drove to the foot of cemetery hill where I knew Donna would give me a hug and a cup of coffee.

Now that the anger was out in the open, the "what-ifs" began crowding into my thoughts with unrelenting force. I found myself dwelling on W. C.'s last few hours. I wondered if he had lain awake pondering things that were heavy on his mind as he retired for the night. I hoped he hadn't felt pain. I wished I had been awake when he had gotten up to start the day. I wondered if he had been dizzy when he went downstairs to plug in the coffee pot. I prayed that I had done everything I could to keep him alive and I realized that this was something I'd never know with certainty.

What if I had insisted that he go to the emergency room the night before when he had complained of not feeling well? What if I had called the doctor like I had wanted to? Why did I let him convince me not to do either? And why didn't I make him slow down when I knew he was overextending himself?

Nothing could be changed one iota by worrying. It was counter-productive to dwell on these things, but they kept cropping up. I knew that I couldn't survive the guilt that was building in my consciousness if I didn't forgive myself for anything I failed to do that would have enabled W. C. to live. It was a big order. God and I worked on that one for a long time.

As those "what-ifs" flooded back I'd push them away because I was truly trying to turn them over to God. I'd occupy my mind with a project that had held much interest for me before and promised someday to be a source of pride and joy again. I'd go for a walk or a swim. I'd seek the companionship of a loving friend. I'd remember the health-giving thought that had come to me over and over—while I didn't have a chance to say goodbye, thank God I didn't really need it. There had been many opportunities to let W. C. know how proud I was to be his wife, and I had taken advantage of them often. This was a guilt I didn't have to bear.

Weary from worry, I determined to stage a counterattack. Mom and I decided to take a trip. Venturing out on our own was something we found to be intimidating. Though we were no strangers to travel, doing so without W. C. was embarking on an uncharted course. Mom wanted to visit her sister, Ruth, in Louisiana, so we bought airline tickets and

THE ANGER, THE GUILT, THE "WHAT-IFS" 83

started planning. I still can't believe that I buckled that seat belt and allowed myself to be transported above the clouds—I, who had steadfastly refused to look down upon the Alps or the Grand Canyon! It was such a joy to see Mom's enthusiasm. I was glad we had made the effort.

Back home, I continued that counterattack. I needed a little pampering and, by golly, I was worth it. I began to take time for luxurious bubble baths and facial treatments. I started an exercise regimen, walking, swimming, and working out on the machines that heretofore came to my attention only when I fell over them. I worked on my diet, eliminating fats where possible and including all of the needed nutrients and fiber. I had a make-up and color analysis, then bought cosmetics and clothing in my colors. I tried a new hairstyle and exotic colognes. I even got sculptured fingernails.

I spruced up my living room, planted a flower and vegetable garden and some shrubbery. We went to Norfolk to visit my son, Bill, and to Alexandria to visit my sister, Joy, and Atlanta to visit my daughter, Linda, and her family. We also made plans that included additional travel. We went to the mall, shopped awhile and saw a movie. I crawled into bed at night with a good book or watched a television program that held interest for me. There was time for work, but I also saw to it that I had time for relaxation and just goofing off if that's what pleased me.

I built up my self-esteem by tackling things I had always left for W. C. I hung pictures, kept the car in good repair, conducted bank business, and equipped my medicine cabinet so that an emergency trip to town could be avoided. I made a list of jobs I couldn't handle by myself and delegated them to others. I became cognizant of potential danger and had an electrical appliance protector and a water heater safety valve installed. I chose to take communion at the front of the church since I no longer had the safety of W. C.'s arm to help me up and down the steps to the altar.

I bought a back scratcher. I gave away our "look alike" clothing. I consoled myself with the knowledge that W. C. could never be hurt again—not by failure of someone to live up to his expectations, not by falling asleep at the wheel of the car because he was so exhausted, not by any of the things I had been prone to worry about when he was alive. I realized with relief that I'd never have to experience his death again.

Because he would not be there to care for me in illness or old age, I began planning for these eventualities, letting my children know my wishes in the matters.

I gave myself permission to buy the easier to use rolls of regular stamps at Christmas time rather than the sheets of holiday stamps W. C. had always purchased far in advance.

I threw open the drapes each morning so the sunshine could flood into my life. I was ultimately responsible for my own happiness and I was the only one who could turn the sadness into purposeful living. I was a survivor!

The anger, the guilt and the "what-ifs"—I seldom think about them anymore. They were a part of the grief process that I found excruciatingly painful, but they were also avenues of healing. I am glad that they finally surfaced so that I could deal with them. And I am grateful for God's leading as I struggled through this phase of the journey upon which we had embarked.

CHAPTER IX

WORK ETHIC OR WORKAHOLIC?

"For we are labourers together with God: ye are
God's husbandry, ye are God's building."
(1 Corinthians 3:9)

HE prerequisite for survival required me to examine all aspects of my situation and to deal with them to the best of my ability. I couldn't sweep anything under the rug and hope it would not intrude on my quest for healing. So I stripped to the bone and laid bare the whole question of work ethic and the workaholic. I believe this to be a matter of concern to many clergy families. The time that had elapsed since W. C.'s death had brought me some measure of understanding, but I still had ambivalent feelings about work schedules as they relate to one's physical well-being and the well-being of one's family. This was a problem that we, as well as many of our friends, had struggled with on a daily basis. There was no easy solution for us—not one that was joint and acceptable, that is.

In my sleepless nights following W. C.'s death I would cry out, "Why?" The week before he died I had said to him, "Honey, if you don't slow down Emory & Henry will have to do without you forever—and so will I!" As he grew older he had taken on more and more. It was almost as if he had to get everything in place before retirement years descended upon him. Retirement was an ogre breathing down his neck and he wanted none of it. Fourteen to sixteen hour days, six to seven day weeks and vacations only to attend work-related events were the norm for him. He became so weary he could hardly put one foot in front of the other when he finally allowed himself the luxury of falling into bed at night. W. C. was an optimist. He had always been able to accomplish anything he set out to do. He had more energy than anyone I've ever known and only in recent years had the stress and strain of his strenuous living begun to take a toll.

I was worried about him. I knew that he could not keep up the pace he had set for himself. I also knew that he would never change. My mind was preoccupied with thoughts of his impending death—not overt thoughts, but fleeting glimpses of a future without him. At a funeral of one of our friends, just a month before W. C. died, I remember putting myself in the widow's place and wondering how I could ever manage the mechanics of a visitation—standing for hours, recalling names, and making introductions. And for several years I had sat through the conference sessions where retirees and their spouses had their say, trying to imagine what I'd come up with and drawing a complete blank. When we took the decorations down after the Christmas that turned out to be his last, I was despondent. He mentioned that he'd need to rebuild the shed for our outdoor manger scene next year. There was a heavy feeling in my heart as the thought kept recurring—what if he's not here next year?

Did I subconsciously know that W. C. could not live with the kind of pressures he had heaped on himself? Was God preparing me for the worst? Or was it a combination of the two? I don't know.

W. C. knew that I feared for his health, but he didn't realize that he was undermining it. Oh, how I wish he had not worked until he collapsed. I wish he had known and accepted his physical limitation. I wish he had taken time to swim, to walk and to play tennis or golf, or just to relax. Did God's laws of nature dictate the outcome of a life lived without thought of personal well-being? Knowing the answer wouldn't change anything. I try not to dwell on these thoughts.

W. C. also knew that I wanted more of his time for myself. Through the years I had pressed for this for our family. I truly tried to effect these changes, but I was unable to do so.

He was such a giving person. There was no attempt to impress, no pretense, no thought of personal gain. He loved life and he put every ounce of vitality, care and concern he could muster into his daily existence. He was the gentle peacemaker who took into his world an adopted daughter, a foster daughter, an invalid father-in-law, an elderly mother-in-law and an aunt by marriage. He did it for me, yes, but he did it also because he truly wanted to. He referred to us as "his girls" and he showered us with love and compassion.

"To what do you attribute W. C.'s vitality and zest for living?" a friend asked me one day. I didn't know the answer until after his death when I learned that his mother had dedicated him to God before he was born. What a heritage; what a responsibility!

And herein lies my ambivalence. It was comforting to know that he touched so many lives and helped so many people. I truly do understand that something within him drove him to do anything he thought needed to be done. No task was too menial. A few days before his death he was seen dusting the piano as people gathered for a concert at the chapel. The piano needed dusting and he was the one who noticed it. There was nothing unusual in that, for he gave with no thought of appropriateness, monetary return or glory.

I was proud of his accomplishments, but I also wished with all of my heart that he had delegated something along the way so that he could have spent more time with us. He couldn't seem to ask others to assume responsibilities he considered to be his. Maybe, just maybe, if he had paced himself he'd have had twenty or thirty more years to give to those persons and causes he felt compelled to embrace—and we would have had those wonderful years together. He might still be here for me, for the rest of his family, for his college and students and for his church. But because I couldn't modify his work habits and because I knew how much that work meant to him, I accepted them as an integral part of this wonderful man.

A memo he attached to his last contract stated, "I am just as excited about signing this contract as I was about signing my first one in 1956." A search of my innermost heart reassures me that he did what he thought was best. He lived his life in the glory of God's calling. He died, as he always wanted to die, giving until he had nothing left to give. He had committed himself to a life of service; he fulfilled what he perceived to be his mission with distinction and integrity.

I have found peace in knowing that he treasured every minute of his hectic day and that he was truly fulfilled. I have to keep reminding myself of this, however, as I look ahead to retirement years alone.

I've tried to deal with these vacillating thoughts. I've given each one its moment of consciousness, analyzed it and lived with it for a while until it became a part of my experience. There are moments when I find two vastly opposite feelings clamoring for recognition. How can I be disappointed that W. C. didn't slow down so he could continue to live and share our ministry and at the same time feel pride in what he accomplished for God as he zoomed through life ministering to the needs of others? It's mind-boggling. It is also a moot question for my family and me at this point in time.

But it might not be so for many of you readers. I hope you will pore over these next few pages with an open mind and an open heart. They're meant to help you examine your own values and put into perspective your own needs and those of your family.

Is the word "workaholic" ever used to describe you? If so, do you smile, at least inwardly, with the satisfaction of knowing that folks recognize your ability to get things done and to make a difference in the world in which you live? Let's go one step further. Being a devoted worker is good. The ability to do one's job well, vital interest and concern for others, willingness to work hard and to give of yourself, integrity to your commitment and calling—these are all wonderful assets. The person who possesses them is a success. Webster defines work ethic as "the belief that work is morally good." Along with the workaholic, most of us have this belief.

But the workaholic becomes a compulsive worker, and this is what I want you to think about now. Amid the press of responsibilities, the constant demands, the oppressive schedule, do you take time for yourself and your family? I know that even the best laid plans can, and will, go awry. If a meeting of genuine importance, a funeral or an emergency counseling need arises on your day off, do you schedule another day for yourself as soon as possible? Or, do you just shrug your shoulders and think, no rest for the weary. An even worse scenario, do you *have* a day off?

Do you suffer from the inability to say no to yet another request that intrudes on your time and pushes aside the things in your personal life that may be even more important? Okay, so you don't want to say no. Then don't. Say instead, "I'm sorry that I can't speak at your luncheon because we have some family plans. I'd be glad, however, to suggest someone else who will do a good job for you. I'll let him/her know you'll be calling, if you wish." Or, "Yes, I'd like to work with you on that project, but I can't see you tomorrow. Would three o'clock on Tuesday be okay?" Most people will understand and respect these decisions.

I am not pleading with you to renege on your job responsibilities or to neglect your work. Rather, I am imploring you to set priorities while you still can. Do your job with integrity; give it your best. But, don't let it become all-consuming to the detriment of your health and the exclusion of your family.

I don't think that God wants this kind of allegiance. He expects us to take advantage of all that He has provided for us in this world—to rejoice in human relationships, to savor the beauty of nature, to find pride and joy in meaningful pursuits, whether they be recreation, study, worship or work-related. He expects us to strike our own balance after careful consideration and prayerful petitions for guidance. If all that is precious to you is wiped out in one terrible moment, would you spend the rest of your life regretting missed opportunities? Is what you are so busy doing today, as tremendously important as it truly is, worth what you might never again have the opportunity to experience?

Why don't you put this book down—right now—and make a date with your spouse. Take your children to a ball game, reschedule that meeting so you will be able to attend the father/son or mother/daughter banquet. Take action to change the direction of your lifelong training and habits. Take control of your life and live it as you plan to live it when the pressures and demands are no longer so immediate. Believe me—for I know—life can be snatched away in a blink of an eye and there is no turning back.

If you aren't convinced yet, consider this. When you are no longer able to do all of the things you feel compelled to do, someone will step in and take over. You are not indispensable—invaluable, perhaps—but not indispensable to your chosen profession. Your superiors might think they can't get along without you. They might, indeed, find it almost impossible to do so, but they will eventually carry on. Several people might replace you, your work might be farmed out to other departments, but the transition will be accomplished and you will no longer be needed. This is the way it must be. You were young once, clamoring for a start so you could grow into the seasoned, invaluable worker you are today. You probably found yourself replacing someone who had come to the time of retirement or who had gone on to the better world. You will not be forgotten, but you *will* be replaced. Other teachers will stand before your students. Other doctors and dentists will care for your patients. Other lawyers will argue your cases in court. Other ministers will preach from your pulpits.

So don't dream about taking that trip together someday. Don't put off celebrating the little things that are special to your relationship until you have more time. Make time now; tomorrow could be too late. Do all that is within your power to sustain physical and emotional health by cutting down on stress-related activities. Perhaps, then, it will not be necessary for others to assume responsibilities within your family that are now yours.

It is easy to be a workaholic. Most of us can spot these tendencies in our own lives. If we recognize these behaviors, however, we can also change them. Coping with grief has taught me to be good to myself. If I spend half of the night writing on a manuscript, I sleep in the next morning. I can also lay it aside in order to spend time with friends or do something that will give me pleasure. I am more relaxed and can handle the stress of daily living better if I have also encountered its joys and its pleasures.

William A. Miller in *The Joy of Feeling Good*, lists eight ways to help you live your own life. I was particularly impressed by the eighth, "Take time to smell the flowers." He goes on to say, "As you live your own life, make sure that you take time to have fun, to play, to let the child in you romp freely, to refresh, and to recreate. Do it! If you must, write it into your schedule. But do it. Take time to smell the flowers."[1]

Work ethic? Yes, I truly do believe that work is morally good! Workaholic? Never again! Why should I destroy my work ethic by letting work dominate my entire life?

W. C. WITH WORK-STUDY STUDENTS— JENNY REDMOND LUCAS AND BRIAN TAYLOR

CHAPTER X

SPECIAL DAYS—A YEAR OF "FIRSTS"

"I can do all things through Christ
which strengtheneth me."
(Philippians 4:13)

HE anticipation of pain as we face days that have special meaning for our families can be overwhelming. We dread each event as it approaches, put off dealing with it for as long as we can, then finally devise our own method of confronting it.

We push ourselves at times to do the traditional, especially when drastic change would be a great struggle for others. But even in these instances, moderate changes are possible and the give and take of retaining old traditions and at the same time developing new ones can be a challenge.

Living without W. C. was agonizing. On special days the distress was compounded. There were thoughts of what we had done in the past, visions of what we might be doing had he lived, and an aching emptiness as I realized over and over again that these celebrations were no longer a part of our life; they would have to be changed, modified, adapted to fit into my life.

Easter was the first holiday I faced without him. The sunrise service was held in the cemetery, close to his grave. This beautiful spot overlooking the campus held a peculiar fascination for me. I was grateful that the children had come home to be with us.

Father's Day came next, but I no longer had a dad of my own or the father of my children to pamper. It was hard.

What would have been our forty-fourth wedding anniversary was a dreary day, the kind that tends to dispense gloom, even if there is something to celebrate. When the poignant memories pressed into my consciousness I relived that long ago event that marked the beginning of our life together and I thanked God for each of those wonderful years.

The children called to let me know that I was in their thoughts and prayers. How does one survive grief without this kind of support?

I can sit here and wallow in self-pity or I can pull out the manuscript I've been writing and do something constructive, I admonished myself. I worked on the manuscript all day. I won't say that wishful thoughts didn't intrude on my attempt to keep busy; they did. I kept thinking of my sister, Shirley, and her husband, Milton, who had shared our double wedding. Both of them were dead, also. I was the lone survivor and I missed the others terribly.

But the sadness didn't take over. When the day was finished I could honestly say that it wasn't as bad as I had feared. Mom and I were visiting my sister, Joy, and her husband, Bud, who had been our staunch supporters through this grief journey. We went out for supper that night. It helped.

W. C. would have celebrated his sixty-fifth birthday the next month. I went with friends on an all-day shopping trip, focused on activities of the moment, and got through the day with a minimum of trauma.

But the next special day, just three weeks later, promised to be the one that would do me in! It was Mom's birthday, and for several years we had hosted a weekend reunion for all of our family. We had rented a dorm at the college for additional sleeping space and had the cafeteria cater meals.

Special Days—A Year of "Firsts"

The special birthday dinner had been elaborately done at one of the beautiful campus locations. W. C. had been in his glory as master of ceremonies for the occasion. Skits were prepared by the great-grandchildren, presents were opened, and Mom ended the evening by gathering her "greats" around her and giving them each a crisp new dollar bill. This yearly birthday party was something she looked forward to with eager anticipation. It was a festive, dress-up occasion, which was a delight to my mom who loved festive, dress-up occasions.

AT GRANDCHICK'S BIRTHDAY PARTY.
ANN, JONATHAN, W. C., LAURA LEE, LAURA RUTH,
LINDA, GRANDCHICK, BILL, KEN, ZACHARY

Time was growing short and I knew that I had to start making preparations. I'd go into my office and mutter, "Why can't I dig into these tasks with Mason gusto? W. C. would have cleared them up in no time flat?" I needed to call the cafeteria and college office, but we had always done that together. I couldn't dial those numbers and set up appointments to discuss catering and housing arrangements. I had files with past years' menus. I knew where we had slept each family member. I just couldn't deal with the reunion and it was almost upon us.

Because Mom looked forward to the occasion so much, I determined not to let her down. So we talked about what we could do to incorporate changes into this annual event, changes that would make hosting it possible for me and enjoying it assured for her. We compromised, deciding to keep everyone at the house, pitching tents in the back yard for the children. The birthday dinner was still catered, as were other meals, but it was a less formal "at home" occasion. The children enjoyed this tremendously because they didn't have to dress up. I suspect that Mom was a little disappointed—for the exact same reason. But, we had a celebration and her family surrounded her with love. And I did the best I could. Oh, how I wish I had been able to manage the elaborate weekend for her, but I knew that she understood my inability to do so and she accepted it with good grace.

The distress I felt as Halloween approached took me by surprise. This was not one of the holidays W. C. had been involved in with any regularity. He usually had a meeting or was out of town. When the children were small I had helped them carve jack-o-lanterns, decorate the house, give out treats, and make the rounds of the neighborhood. However, last year W. C. had been home to answer the door. He had enjoyed seeing each group of goblins, filling their trick or treat bags, and showing them the Halloween tree we had created together. It was a wonderful night, the only Halloween in my recent memory that he had been a part of. Would I have put the tree up again? I don't know. Halloween was spent with Linda and her family in Atlanta—among their customs and traditions, and I didn't have to face that decision.

The Thanksgiving and Christmas holidays were approaching and I was tormented by the desire to go away somewhere until they were over. I had gotten through the other special days, but the dread of facing this time of year was debilitating. I knew I couldn't take a trip; I had seriously considered it, but I needed my family, and they needed me. They were already facing the season without their dad. I tried to pretend that the joyous activities were not going on, but they were all around me. Everyone was happy it seemed except me. How I wished that I could just go to sleep and wake up when it was all over. That, too, was impossible.

I bombarded God with pleas for help. Life had lost its zest and I needed enthusiasm to face the holiday season. "Please, God, don't let me fall apart now," I begged. "I feel so helpless and alone. I've tumbled from the bandwagon of life and everyone is going on without me." Even in this most anguished hour I felt God's presence and knew that I wasn't truly alone. I also knew that nobody could climb back on that bandwagon for me. Step by step I'd have to make that ascent on my own. I reminded myself that I was a survivor. I didn't rush joyously into the dreaded season, but I simplified preparations when I could. I accepted the fact that no amount of pretending would make me happy, so I gave myself permission to grieve, to have sad thoughts, to cry if I needed to. But I also resolved to wade into the next four or five weeks with a determination to find some smattering of happiness.

The children and grandchildren joined us for Thanksgiving, as did Joy and Bud and my nieces, Cheryl and Kay. We started a new tradition, a suggestion we received from the Holiday Help Seminar sponsored by Farris Funeral Home. We lit a candle in remembrance of loved ones who were no longer with us and offered a prayer of thanksgiving for each one. With tearful eyes we started our meal, but it wasn't long until favorite stories began to surface. We found ourselves remembering the warm, cozy and funny things that had endeared each one of them to us.

With that many people to feed, keeping busy was no chore. By the same token, we had added hands to help with whatever needed doing and I gratefully accepted all offers. I got through the day better than I had hoped. I was thankful for family who cared enough to be there for me.

The Christmas season fused itself into the Thanksgiving celebration even earlier than it had the year before. I cringed when I heard carols, carols I had always loved. The bright lights reminded me of happier days. Our home had always stood out like a sore thumb at Christmas time. W. C. concocted an elaborate electrical system that allowed him to have red candles in every window, and three gleaming trees throughout the house—one with nothing but strawberry ornaments, most of which had been given to him by students who knew of his absolute passion for strawberries. The brilliantly illuminated shrubbery in the front yard served as a backdrop for the life-sized manger scene. Memories of him rushing home each evening and going from room to room creating his own little "red light district" were poignant. I knew that I could not put all of that up; I probably never would, but student groups were coming for parties and we had to be decorated.

I needed to put the manger scene outside and I *knew* I couldn't do it. Why, the shed was in scraps all over my basement. I would have to carry them up piece-by-piece and construct it in the bitter cold. I contemplated not displaying it, but I couldn't do that either. W. C. and I had found great pleasure and meaning in gazing upon those lighted figures last year and felt that others had found it a source of inspiration also. I got the hammer and nails and put that shed together. I hooked up the electrical system to light the figures and then I came to the star. When I tried it in the indoor plugs, it shone brightly. When I took it outside, climbed the ladder and attached it to the tree limb, the lights went out. Over and over I brought it in, then took it out again. My knees were throbbing and my fingers too numb to feel, when a friend called and asked what I was doing. My heated reply has become legend throughout the community and though this story is remembered, the real meaning of the manger scene continues to fill the hearts of those who see it and worship the baby who came to earth so that we could be forgiven!

I awakened one morning to find that fierce winds and heavy ice had toppled the manger scene. This was the last straw. I slipped a rope around the shed, pulled it upright, and tied it to a nearby tree. Looking up into the ugly gray clouds, I declared, "I took care of it, honey," then rushed back into the warmth of the house to escape the wintry blast.

Life all around us was festive, but my heart still ached as I faced this first Christmas without W. C. "Oh, God," I prayed, "W. C. and I are separated this Christmas, but we won't always be, for I claim your promise, 'whosoever believeth in Him shall not perish, but have ever-lasting life.' I do believe."

Christmas was spent in Atlanta with Linda and her family. It was hard being there without W. C. But, away from my familiar routines I found it easier to face the holidays. We had our customary Christmas Eve service. I was grateful that the children had remembered their dad's memorial candle.

Christmas morning was wonderfully hectic, as it always had been. And dinner with Bud and Nina Ruth, Ken's folks, was a joy. They, too, had a memorial candle. I went to bed that night with a prayer of gratitude in my heart. I had gotten through the day, and it hadn't been nearly as bad as I had feared. It really hadn't.

New Year's Eve followed. I missed our group of friends who usually celebrated this night together, but I was grateful that I had been included so graciously in my daughter's and son-in-law's circle of friends.

Valentine's day will always be associated with W. C.'s death. We had gone to a banquet for our district ministers and their spouses. It was a lovely affair, but W. C. had to rush back to campus after introducing our chaplain, who was the speaker. He disappeared through the door saying, "I've already heard this speech." His remarks elicited a laugh from the group, probably the last laugh any of them shared with him. Three days later his rushing ceased. As the anniversary of this day approached I couldn't help but wonder if things might have been different if he had formed the habit of having someone else introduce the film to students who waited as he flew back to campus and dashed up the stairs to the auditorium.

The last "first" that had to be faced was the anniversary of W. C.'s death. Having become a veteran at facing special days, I determined to do the things that had helped me most as I journeyed through the year—staying close to my Heavenly Father, keeping busy at something that was meaningful, and finding solace in the company of family and friends who understood me and were comfortable with my grief process. It was a busy day; it was a sad day, but it was not devastating. I had finally reached the end of the first year and I had survived!

In looking back I realized that we spent about two-thirds of these special days at home and the other third away. This was not by design, but it seemed to be a good mix. Sometimes it was helpful to get into another routine and at other times the familiar, with a certain amount of modification, was best. In any event, we were not left alone; our family either called or came and we felt their support as we encountered these particularly difficult occasions.

I was surprised by the fact that, in almost every instance, the dread far surpassed the actual pain. The pain was compounded by the many useless hours I had spent dealing with its anticipation.

For the rest of my life there will be moments when grief will engulf me. Birthdays, holidays and anniversaries will bring back memories. W. C. will be missed at weddings of the grandchildren and baptisms of the great-grandchildren. There will be a peculiar sadness in all of these happy, momentous occasions because he would have been such a vital part of them.

We will see that the great-grandchildren grow up knowing about him. What a loss that they will never actually experience his physical presence. I've turned that over to God, also, and I am confident that my longing for W. C.'s participation in these future events will not mar the experience for my loved ones or me.

Though grief is not logical, there are times, even during the grief process, when one must make a conscious effort to weigh both sides of a situation and come up with a logical plan of action. Barry Neil Kaufman, through his book, *Happiness Is a Choice*, helped me look at the whole idea of happiness once more. Happiness truly is a choice. I had already determined that I was going to make a concerted effort to recover this elusive emotion. But, as in all stages of my grief process, I had wavered. Kaufman's statement, "Happiness and the belief that we can experience our own happiness, any time and any place, is the ultimate attitudinal advantage,"[1] made sense to me. Attitudes are important, I thought. Great. I'm dealing with an attitude now—I can do something about that.

W. C. AFTER THE BAPTISM OF OUR FIRST GRANDCHILD—LAURA RUTH

CHAPTER XI

I'M BEGINNING TO HEAL

"But they that wait upon the Lord shall renew their strength; they shall mount up with wings as eagles; they shall run and not be weary; and they shall walk, and not faint."
(Isaiah 40:31)

 CAME to a time in our journey when I desperately wanted to feel good again. And so I started searching the shelves for books whose central theme did not necessarily speak to the grief process, but to the fullness of life available before, during, after and even if no grief experience had befallen. I found help in Dr. Norman Vincent Peale's *The Power of Positive Living*. He described a feeling of gloom that prevailed over a dinner party conversation about a faltering community project. A person who seldom spoke came up with the comment, "Things may look bad, but . . ." Dr. Peale went on to say that after a silence various possibilities were projected by those present, and they began looking at the situation in a positive manner. "To me," he continued, "it was an incident of enormous import. For I saw the immense positive power in the common three-letter word but. It says that the situation, bleak as it may appear, is not all that bad. There is hope. There are possibilities."[1] I came away from the reading of that book looking for the possibilities in my life.

My world was still in disarray, but I was beginning to feel a little less lonely. The pain was not as sharp, the hurt dulled. Accepting the reality that our marriage was over continued to be the hardest task I had ever set for myself. Perhaps this was so because we had experienced such a special relationship. I found myself remembering the good times, but even an ideal marriage has its ups and downs; I thought about the latter also. Why was I remembering the negatives when I really didn't want to? I had a feeling that they had to come into my consciousness so that I could deal with them and then put them to rest.

While I wished I had handled some situations differently, I knew with all of my heart that my behavior was part of a sound and happy marriage, and that in 99% of the instances, given a second opportunity, I would have repeated that behavior. There were sometimes twinges of regret, sometimes a chuckle or two. I won a few, he won a few, and there had been a lot of compromise. It was important for me to recognize that differences were inevitable, that they were a natural part of the blending process as two personalities came together with ideas, philosophies and habits gleaned from separate life experiences. These differences didn't weaken the marriage. They were strengthening threads, interwoven with others of equal strength and fused into a unifying tapestry. The "downs" in our life had added growth and stability, the "ups" happiness without measure!

Now that I had come to terms with this, I needed to press on with the business of giving up that which was no longer mine.

W. C.'s absence had created such a void in my life. I continued to reach out for him, but felt nothing. Then a situation that would have given him great concern developed in the life of a close friend. I didn't even go to bed the night he came to share it with me. I sat up on the sun porch praying. When I got tired of talking to God I started talking to W. C., all the while thinking that this was a theologically unsound practice. Suddenly I felt a great urgency to go into W. C.'s study. My eyes fell immediately upon a little prayer book he had used when he was a student. Chills went up and down my spine when it opened to *A Prayer For Fortitude*. Was he sending us a message? When I gave this book to our friend the next day we noticed that the prayer on the facing page was W. C.'s favorite, "Lord, make us instruments of your peace . . .." Of course, the logical answer was that the book opened to that page because it had been opened to the precise spot so many times in the past. But why did I feel such an urgency to go into the study at 3:00 a.m. and why did my eyes fall immediately upon that little book? It had been there for years and I scarcely remember noticing it.

I was still pondering these questions and not daring to hope that what I wanted so desperately could be possible when I received a call from Bishop Hunt. His affirmation that my faith was not simplistic—that my beliefs were not unlike those who had studied theology a great deal more than I—was reassuring. But his statement, "I believe W. C. knows we are having this conversation," was the turning point in my grief process. In that very instant I not only felt closer to God, but I found W. C. again. I was beginning to heal!

Bishop Hunt's next statement was electrifying. "W. C. is not devastated about this situation," he assured me. "He sees with different eyes now; he can see the whole picture and he knows that things are going to work out." And they did—not the way I wanted, not the way our friend wanted—but nevertheless a good solution developed.

A few weeks later Mom and I visited a nearby church. It was the first time we had been away from our own church since W. C.'s death, fifteen months earlier. Filling the pulpit was a college senior who had recently married and was going away to seminary. Oh, I thought, what I would give to be starting on that wonderful adventure again—anticipating the tumultuous joys and oblivious of the pitfalls that sometimes crop up along the way. I was deeply moved by his sincerity and more than a little envious of the life that lay ahead of him.

Come on, gal, cut it out, I thought. You had your day and you loved every minute of it. Don't begrudge this young couple theirs.

"Oh, God," I prayed, "I don't like feeling sorry for myself. Please open up new areas of service for me and help me to get on with the business of living. I can't go back and I *know* it, so why do I continue to torture myself with these longings?"

I had accepted the fact that W. C. was dead. I knew I couldn't change that, but I couldn't seem to get beyond the longings, to think about the past without them. I wanted to be able to look forward to the future with enthusiasm. "Give me purpose, God," I continued. "Help me evaluate rationally the options that keep cropping up and choose from them those which are pleasing in Your sight."

Dealing with grief is confusing and disconcerting. Depression and loneliness continue to plague us. Even after we have reached acceptance of our situation we find it difficult to be enthusiastic. But if we put forth the tremendous effort it takes to move beyond this depression, we will be on our way to reentering life, not as it used to be, but as it is now. We must look for and be open to opportunities when they present themselves.

One of my first such ventures was connected to the College. Alumni Day was coming and I toyed with the idea of offering to host my class reunion. Our house was large enough. We had hosted both W. C.'s and mine in the past, but I wasn't sure I could do it without him. You'll never know if you don't try, I told myself, so I made the call that obligated me to the reunion. I needed to get back into doing the things that had always brought me pleasure. I also needed to recommit my time, my energies and my home to worthwhile endeavors. Though I never expected to equal the legacy that W. C. had left, I wanted my little world to be a better place because I had been there. I wanted to make my own difference. I also knew that W. C. was not sitting around on his laurels waiting for me to join him. He was feverishly working for his Lord and I didn't want to be out of practice. I was glad that I had made the effort. I enjoyed having the group in my home. I was beginning to heal!

Perhaps because I was thinking about W. C., I found him in my dreams that night. The smile that radiated from his face seemed to engulf his whole being. His smiles had been legendary, and while they brightened my existence for more than two thirds of my life, I had never before encountered such brilliance. I thanked God for this experience and climbed out of bed to face a rainy, but glorious day!

I turned the television on and saw President Carter hammering away at a Habitat For Humanity project. "Jimmy Carter doesn't even know that W. C.'s dead." I heard myself utter with complete seriousness. My astonishment gave way to a hearty laugh as I realized the ridiculousness of what I had just said. Jimmy Carter didn't even know W. C. had ever existed. But that wasn't important. The realization that I could be amused, that I could find something funny enough to elicit a laugh, even if it was at my own expense, was earth shaking. I was beginning to heal!

The funny things that W. C. was prone to do began flooding back into my memory and, much to my surprise, rollicking, boisterous laughs would rock my whole being. He loved to tell a story and was a master at embellishment. More often than not he was the object of his own ridicule. His jokes were sometimes funny, always corny, and he laughed with such abandon that you had to do likewise. I missed that laughter. I missed seeing him tickle himself under the arm in an effort to solicit a response from others. But I could relive these moments with friends who enjoyed reliving them also. And I could set my imagination soaring as I contemplated which story he might be telling at the moment and who might be in his bemused audience. I also had a strong conviction that at some point in time—God's time—I would again hear his discourse on the mishap of falling down on the way to the pulpit in his new shoes. This one had gotten better with each telling. I'd have no concern about turning blue or trying to breathe between gales of laughter and there would be no need to summon a doctor to control my spiraling heartbeat. Truly Heaven is a marvelous place. Streets of gold? Who needs them? But love, compassion, beauty, companionship, and yes, even humor—all enhanced beyond our wildest dreams—these are ours, freely given by a benevolent God who sent His Son that we might have this wonderful life and that it might be ours for eternity.

I was learning to live without W. C. There were times when the hurt was still overpowering, but there were also times when I actually felt happy. I knew that I would find purpose and fulfillment as life went on. It was gratifying that pleasure was beginning to manifest itself in my daily experiences. I was glad that I could laugh at a joke and remember W. C.'s lovable antics with amusement. I had almost forgotten this part of him. What a pity.

The realization that I hadn't cried in a long time suddenly dawned upon me. I can begin wearing eye make-up again,

I thought, as if that was of importance. What *was* important was that I was beginning to heal.

I was grateful to W. C., whose constant compliments had helped me affirm my self-worth. I couldn't deal with a lifetime of being without him just yet, but God had given me strength to face being without him today.

About this time I came across two framed sayings that gave me a chuckle as I digested their message. The first was a picture of Hagar the Horrible, of comic strip fame. With arms raised in supplication as a fierce storm raged around him he exclaimed, "Why me?" and a voice from Heaven boomed out with the astonishing counter-question, "Why *not*?" Dick Browne's humor had touched my funny bone and I laughed out loud.

The second was a counted cross-stitch picture of a cute little sad-faced bear, her empty fishing pole dangling from a row boat. "If today were a fish I would throw it back," the caption read. I bought that one for a friend who had lost her husband. "We all have days we'd like to throw back, but thank goodness we also have happy, fulfilling ones," I wrote. "When we can face the sad days with humor, we are beginning to heal."

Dedication of the Emory & Henry Yearbook to W. C. and his Administrative Assistant Dot Culberson. The first of three such dedications to W. C.

Left to right—W. M. Booth, student, Dot Culberson, Dean Lyles, student, W. C.

CHAPTER XII

DOES GOD ANSWER PRAYER? YOU BET!

"But my God shall supply all your need according
to his riches in glory by Christ Jesus."
(Philippians 4:19)

DREAMED of W. C. again a few weeks later. We were at a conference going into our hotel room to rest before supper. Everything was normal—even to the pain in my hip and leg that I experience when I am on my feet more than usual. I awakened with a start to realize that the pain was real. I had forgotten to take the preventive dose of aspirin. But the rest of my dream would never materialize. My first reaction was to thank God for those precious moments that had seemed so real, so happy and so satisfying.

An overpowering sadness suddenly engulfed me, tearing my peace to shreds. I tried to push it away, but the gloom lingered. Outside it was spitting snow. Occasional gusts of wind tore the few leaves that remained from their branches and sent them plummeting to the ground. The cleansing tears gushed as I cried, "Please, God, help me get through this day." For weeks I had been making steady progress and had felt the healing that was going on in my life. Why, then, did I suddenly revert to the utter despair of this moment?

I wandered about the house, unable to concentrate. I looked at W. C.'s picture on my desk and thought—how can you smile like that when I am so unhappy? The heaviness lifted somewhat at the sight of a nursery catalog. I had been intending to order fall bulbs. "I'll do it right now," I resolved, and scurried to the yard to diagram my flowerbeds. The afternoon sped by as I figured heights, ground spread, color, and need for sun or shade. I pasted the pictures from the catalogue onto my diagram and, satisfied with the results, placed my order. Preparing the ground and planting bulbs were activities I could look forward to as I waited for their arrival. A miracle? Perhaps not, but my friends who know how little I know about flowers would think so. And I, acknowledging my usual lack of interest in such pursuits, was indeed grateful for anything that pulled me from my state of depression and gave me an afternoon filled with purposeful endeavor. Does God answer prayer? You bet!

A few days later I awakened to the sound of rain splashing against the windowpane. It was the kind of day that made me want to curl up under the covers and sleep the hours away. But sleep wouldn't return. A wave of loneliness engulfed me, reaching to the very depths of my being, with utter abandon for my resolve to maintain a positive outlook. "Oh, God, it still hurts," I whispered. "When will the pain go away?" Operating on sheer determination, I threw the blankets aside and propelled myself to the floor. I didn't have to consult the list I had made for just such an occasion. *Lots of Ways to Win* needed revision. It was past time to get this manuscript back on its itinerary. Perhaps the next publisher would accept it. Does God answer prayer? You bet! The manuscript wasn't accepted that time, but it gave me something to engross myself in and it helped strengthen the story so that it would be able to stand up better under the scrutiny of prospective publishers.

Being familiar with the stages of grief is comforting at times like this. If we don't know that long lost laughter and joy can finally surface, only to be obliterated by despondency and gloom, we might doubt our own sanity. And if we aren't aware that others also face these ups and downs as they progress through grief, we might feel that we have been singled out—that life is being grossly unfair and that we are its helpless victims. Knowing that grief comes to all of us, however, doesn't change the outcome. We still revert, momentarily, to earlier stages of this process. We still have to work diligently to overcome its anguish.

Once again, I had reverted. "When will I be able to leave the doom and gloom behind me forever?" I asked. Deep down, I already knew the answer. *Never*, at least not completely, but there was hope. The sadness came less frequently. It was not as intense and it didn't last as long. Does God answer prayer? You bet!

It had been twenty months—almost two years—and meaning and purpose were a part of my life again. All of the things I wanted to accomplish began crowding into my thoughts. I was eager to help build up W. C.'s scholarship and loan funds at the College and to continue to befriend the students. The groups we had welcomed into our home when he was alive belonged to someone else now. Their sponsors knew, however, that my home was open to them. It had been built for that purpose and I wanted to maintain student contact. So they graciously shared the entertainment opportunities with me. I could not carry on W. C.'s ministry to students. That would have been both impossible and inappropriate. But I could accept their friendship and love and offer my own in return.

I also wanted to care for my mom for as long as she needed me. Her health was failing and I longed to return the loving care she had lavished on me.

I was anxious to revise and polish the children's stories in my files and study the publisher's market so I could start them on their way once more. I wanted to give expression to new ideas that were beginning to pop into my mind again. And, I wanted to take the recorded bits and pieces of my grief experiences as I had jotted them down and organize them into a book.

I continued to be active in the Clergy Partners Association, inviting them into my home as I had always done. This was an appropriate extension of my role as a minister's wife because widows were welcome in the group. It gave me great pleasure to be able to keep this vestige of my former life.

I was making progress in establishing a life for myself apart from W. C. but it continued to be an up-hill struggle. Impossible? I certainly had thought so. But God has a way of helping us overcome the impossible. Does God answer prayer? You bet!

Little by little He helped me see new opportunities. Little by little He helped me realize that I could function autonomously. Little by little He opened up new vistas for me. I didn't sit back and wait, however. I had to search my own heart; I had to work to perfect my new and expanding interests. I had to make the effort to go on when everything within me was saying, "You can't." Most of all, I had to lean on God, continue my partnership with Him, and *believe* His promise to be with me, "even to the end of the world." I thought my world had ended that fateful Saturday in February. God knew differently!

My thoughts and feelings were changing. I was becoming another "me." I seemed to be looking on as someone else inhabited my body, thought my thoughts, dreamed my dreams, and went about my everyday activities. Certainly this person's life was different from anything mine had ever been. The familiar lifestyle, the one I had become so comfortable in, was no longer there, nor could it ever be. It was almost like learning to walk again. New patterns were developing, however, and they were beginning to feel "right." Then one day I realized that I didn't hurt as much. The war was not over, but God and I were claiming victory over some of the major skirmishes. Does God answer prayer? You bet!

While visiting with my sister Joy and her husband, Bud, one day we decided to drive up to Pennsylvania to see his parents. They lived in a beautiful retirement home—the kind of place I had always envisioned for W. C. and me when we were no longer able to function completely on our own. Couples in their early retirement years mingled with those who were midway through this journey and those who obviously had senior status. My attention was riveted on a perky little man who had to be in the latter category. He stood out in the crowded dining room like a beacon of light among faraway stars in the night sky. A smile radiated from deep within his emaciated body as he went from table to table with an outstretched hand and a cheerful greeting. Convinced that the gray stubble encircling his shiny baldhead had at one time been red, I stared in awe. The vision of W. C., thirty years hence, was indelibly seared into my imagination.

"Life is not fair," I agonized. "Please, God, help me accept that fact. Take away the longing and the envy that are eating at my heart right now. Replace them with a genuine feeling of happiness for these couples in their golden years and a determination to make the best of my situation, just as the single men and women who also reside in this retirement community are doing." Did God answer that prayer? You bet! Acceptance came, for the moment, at least.

Grief is so unpredictable. On a day-to-day basis I was detecting real progress. Life had gotten easier as I had learned to accept that which I could not change. But God and I couldn't climb straight up that mountain and claim victory. There were still the momentary setbacks and there probably always would be. I knew that as time went on I would be increasingly receptive to my new life. I would even find joy in it. Beautiful memories began flooding back—and I had enough to last a lifetime. Does God answer prayer? You bet!

By this time I was sending manuscripts back out as soon as they were returned. It was always a disappointment to get that 8½ x 11 size envelope with a publisher's name in the upper left-hand corner. But I had learned to take rejections in stride. Another returned manuscript, I'd think. Too bad. Then one day it happened! I received a contract for the publication of *Lots of Ways to Win*. I was elated. I shouted rather irreverently, "We *did* it fellas!" Convinced that my wonderful husband was up there cheering me on I added, "And thank you, honey, for believing in me and encouraging me to follow my dreams." I hurried home to share the news with Mom, complete the contract, and return it to Winston-Derek Publishers, Inc. of Nashville, Tennessee. Thus began the saga of my first publishing experience. Oh, life was beautiful. I never expected to be this happy again. My joy would have been complete if W. C. had been there to share it with me. He had been so supportive of my writing endeavors. Does God answer prayer? You bet! But we have to open our hearts and be receptive to His answer. We have to work diligently to bring about our dreams and we have to accept His timetable. We must also believe that when one door is closed to us, another will be opened.

I had been to visit my sister. I had been to visit my children, but I had absolutely no interest in taking an extended vacation. My routines at home were beginning to feel normal, different from those we had enjoyed as a couple, but they had become my way of living and they brought a measure of happiness and peace.

Vacations were a different matter. I had not gone to a resort, stayed at a motel, walked on the beach, ridden the waves, or eaten at a seaside restaurant for a long time. So, I pushed aside the dread of painful memories that had kept me home and went to the beach with my family.

W. C.'s 67th birthday would have been celebrated within this week. No mention was made of the date. I, too, had done the same thing for Mom when her special days came around. I thought that if she could forget, I should not force a painful reminder on her. I know now that she *never* forgot! She simply let me think I was sparing her.

According to Edwin Shneidman in *Voices of Death*, "The deep capacity to weep for the loss of a loved one and to continue to treasure the memory of that loss is one of our noblest human traits." Oh, how I treasured W. C.'s memory. I ached for his presence, but was able to put the past behind me as we went about creating new experiences. We had a wonderful time, and in the process, we stored up some pretty fantastic scenes for our memory bank. Then, it was time to go home. I dreaded it, as I had every time I had gone away, but I knew that I would be okay. I'd settle back into my routine and life would hold pleasure for me again because I willed it and because I could count on God to help me over the rough spots.

It would have been easier to stay home and avoid these adjustments. I knew instinctively, however, that I would never heal if I didn't work through my grief. Avoiding the difficult was tantamount to giving up. Depriving myself of wholesome and satisfying experiences so I wouldn't have to face the sadness of remembered pleasure would have been self-defeating. Does God answer prayer? You bet!

It may not be the answer we envisioned or wanted. It may not be the solution we came up with as we attempted to bargain with Him. We may not even recognize it as an answer. But God, in all of His wisdom and power, *does* answer our prayers. The question we must ask ourselves is, do we pray for things that He can grant within the realm of His orderly universe and His plan for His children's freedom of choice and creativity?

CHAPTER XIII

DESPITE NEW GRIEF, HEALING GOES ON

"God is our refuge and strength, a very
present help in trouble."
(Psalm 46:1)

S we approached the second anniversary of W. C.'s death, Joy and Bud drove down to be with us. We took Mom out for Valentine's Day dinner. On the way home she suffered a heart attack. Two weeks in and out of intensive care and several heart attacks later my wonderful Mom died. Devastated, I was thrown into the grief process anew. I will always be grateful to our chaplain, David St. Clair, who counseled with her right after she was given the news that she could not get better and to our pastor, Brian Miller and his wife, Mary, who were at her side when she died. Indeed, she had been waiting for them to arrive from out of town before joining my sister, Shirley, whose voice she had been hearing all morning, her husband, Milton, my dad and W. C. What a joyous reunion that must have been!

Mom had been my cherished companion for the two years of my bereavement, a vital source of comfort and strength as I trudged through the ups and downs of trying to create a new life. She was there for me every moment of every day, giving up precious time with Joy and her family to devote to my needs. Her death left me living alone for the first time in my entire life—truly alone. The house was empty. There was no one to share my concerns with on a daily basis—no one to kiss goodnight or wake up to in the morning—no one to sip coffee with over the newspaper. I had no one to care for and there was no one to care for me or to share my innermost thoughts and feelings. For the first time in my life, I had no confidante.

Many widows have to face this reality with the initial blow of losing their husband. I was fortunate to have had this time of adjustment. There were friends, there were family members and there were opportunities to lose myself in purposeful activity. But ultimately, when I went to bed at night and when I awakened in the morning, I was painfully aware that I was living alone. Only God knew the depth of my despair. *Only* God! In my self-pity had I forgotten the one Being in this whole Universe who loved me unconditionally—the one Being who could lift me out of that despair?

"Forgive me, God, for these moments of self-indulgence," I prayed, "and help me reach out for the strength and courage you have provided during these past two years. Enable me to go on in the face of extreme loneliness. Help me to seek out others who are lonely also. Please, God, continue to nurture me and guide me in the paths you would have me go."

Mom and I had grown quite close. She was pretty as a picture with her beautiful gray hair. She wore a bright scarf and earrings to match every outfit and she traipsed around in coordinated sling-back high heels. She was stylishly dressed, even for a picnic. And at ninety-five, she still exhibited the beauty of character that had earned her the nickname, "Grandchick", early in her dealings with her beloved grandchildren. Oh, how I missed her.

I awakened one morning with the words of an old hymn playing over and over in my mind. "He leadeth me: O blessed thought! O words with heavenly comfort fraught! What e'er I do, where e'er I be, still 'tis God's hand that leadeth me." I remembered that the day before had been one of deep depression and loneliness. I had experienced the kind of despair that I had not felt in a long time. Nothing I did helped to pull me out of it. The fact that I was pressured to get some work to my publisher and income tax was breathing down my neck might have precipitated the doom and gloom, but there were other factors at work. I was lost without Mom.

"I've never lived alone, God, and I am so frightened," I prayed. "Thank You for reminding me that even through my deepest gloom, You are there to lead me."

"Count your assets in the face of a bleak situation," Robert H. Schuller said in his book, *Life's Not Fair But God Is Good*. "Now you can see why it's really true: Life's not fair—but God is good"[1] Life *isn't* always fair, but it is consistent. It changes for my acquaintances, my friends and my family—just as it changes for me. There is nothing any of us can do about it, other than to accept the challenge of a new situation and pray for strength to live courageously. The changes that come to us as we grow older don't always bring the kinds of things we have envisioned for ourselves. But, God is there to help us accept our realities and growth is often the by-product of this acceptance—growth, renewal, and direction.

I doubled my efforts to look for the positives in my life. My friends continued to keep me in their care. I lived one day at a time and, with God's help, was able to find something of worth in it. The healing process had suffered a setback, but it continued on its unpredictable journey. And then it happened again. I lost my mother-in-law whom I loved dearly! She had befriended me from the moment we met. I am sure she wondered about this young girl who was planning to marry her son and eventually assume the responsibilities of his parsonage home. But she didn't share her doubts. Many prospective mothers-in-law would have. She upheld us in every decision we made, even when she must have wondered if we had lost our minds. Many mothers-in-law would have spoken out. She was kind and loving to our children and was, in turn, loved by them.

She had been an invalid for more than a year. I treasure the week I was allowed to spend caring for her just a few months before her death. I'd sit by her bed each night until she drifted off to sleep. It was the loneliest time of the day for both of us, so we spent it together. We shared a lifetime of memories. We had talked on the phone nightly since W. C.'s death and the knowledge that I could no longer dial her number and hear her voice on the other end of the line saddened me.

I ran into a friend at the post office one day. With outstretched arms and deep compassion he asked, "How are you, Freddie?"

"I'm all right, Chick," I replied. "I really am!"

It had been only eight months since my mom had died. There was an ache in my heart because I loved them both and an absence in my life that no one else could fill. But I didn't feel that God had sent yet another tragedy on me. Neither did I feel that He was testing my faith. I knew that both of my moms had died because their bodies were worn out. Their death brought relief from suffering, as did that of my dad, my sister and brother-in-law and my father-in-law before them. For this I had to be grateful. It didn't lessen my grief over their death; it made it bearable.

The depth of anguish I was suffering because of my three recent losses could not be measured in a test tube. Neither could my dependence on those loved ones or the void their death had created in my life. Grief had returned with a wallop and I was reeling from its blow.

Death is a part of life and if we live to an age when our loved ones are likely to face it, death will become a force with which we have to reckon over and over again. It is not something to fear or to shrink from. Neither is it punishment. It is simply an orderly process in the experience of life—just as miraculous as birth itself and just as mysterious. Death is a part of God's plan. What lies beyond is also a part of that plan. We don't really need to know how God has worked out the logistics.

Heaven took on a whole new perspective as each one of my loved ones entered its realm. The dread of the unknown vanished and was replaced with an awareness that I, too, will make that journey someday, and, *hey*, it's going to be okay! But, until then I have to work toward conquering each new grief that comes into my life. I might go up one step and slip back two, but I will top that mountain if I dig in and grab the lifeline God holds out to me.

This time it didn't take me as long. I made steady progress as I employed the measures that had helped before and took advantage of the resources that I now knew were available. Despite new grief, the healing process was going on.

PROVIDERS OF ENABLING SUPPORT AND ENABLING LOVE—
OUR MOMS—
MYRTLE MASON AND LAURA FREDERICK

CHAPTER XIV

HAS GOD ABDICATED HIS POSITION OF POWER?

"The God of love and peace shall be with you."
(2 Corinthians 13:11)

OO often we human beings want a miracle. Proving that God exists or that He is powerful demands a supernatural display of power, an eerie manifestation, something dramatic that we can see, hear and feel. But aren't our bodies themselves miracles? From the divine plan an act of love produces human beings, the greatest of God's creations. Though their traits are received from both parents, they are, nevertheless, persons in their own right. They are able to feel a range of emotions, but there is not a physical place we can point to as the site of these feelings. They are able to hear a range of sounds, but how the ear receives and transmits these sounds to the brain is in itself miraculous. They can also see; they can touch; they can taste and they can smell. We take these five senses for granted because they are a part of what we have always known. Think of them; think of them one by one. Is this not our miracle?

God doesn't set us adrift on this planet without a purpose. He hasn't left us to fend for ourselves. He rejoices when we succeed. He cares when we face discouragement and failure, and He is there for us through it all. Strength and courage are ours for the asking. But you say, "I can't see God. I can't hear Him." Of course you can't, if you are expecting a giant in the sky and a thundering voice to boom from the heavens. God *could* do that, but He usually doesn't choose that approach. He responds to our supplications by awakening within our souls a feeling of serenity and peace.

Bishop Earl G. Hunt, Jr., in his book, *I Have Believed*, states, "A Christian is not immune to suffering and tragedy. I have always been grateful that my own belief has been in the kind of God who does not send suffering and tragedy upon his children, but who is able to take such experiences when they come and turn them into something constructive, worthwhile, and even beautiful."[1]

I, also, believe in a God who does not send tragedies upon His children—and in a God who helps us turn the tragedies that become a part of our lives into something "constructive, worthwhile and beautiful."

He gives us the freedom of choice, however, that sometimes gets us into trouble. And He allows us to live in a beautiful universe whose laws of nature cannot be compromised. God hurts along with us when we suffer because of our own actions or those of others and when we become victims of natural forces over which we have no control.

Harold Kushner, in speaking about the Holocaust says, "I have to believe that the Holocaust was at least as much of an offense to God's moral order as it is to mine . . ." He goes on to say in his book, *When Bad Things Happen To Good People*, that in order for God to let us be free, He has to let us choose right or wrong—good or evil. But Rabbi Kushner states that God also feels anguish and compassion, sympathy and outrage.[2]

Has God, then, abdicated His position of power? I believe not. He could direct our every move, step in and neutralize danger, control the universe with an iron fist. But we would then be as robots, robbed of the satisfaction of accomplishment. There would be no need for us to think, to feel, to strive for excellence. Life would be dull and unattractive. We would have no chance for growth, no self-worth, no reason to put forth our best effort or to help others. We would be nothing more than cogs in the machinery of life, performing with predictable ease and boredom. There would be no right or wrong, no good or evil. We would be deprived of the feeling of euphoria. There would be no sorrow, it is true, but could we experience joy if we had not also known sorrow? Could we grow if we had no place of beginning?

I believe that God is capable of anything He deems good or right, but He usually limits direct intervention in favor of letting us become creative individuals. When we exercise our choices we sometimes set into motion a series of cause and effect relationships. If we choose to use tobacco or eat fatty food we can expect to substantially increase our chances of catastrophic illness on down the road. If we choose to volunteer our time to a worthy cause we can expect to see tangible benefits for the recipient of our labors plus a sense of satisfaction for ourselves.

Has God abdicated His position of power? No. God is the master of delegation. He could bring into being a cure for cancer, stop a war or direct the course of negotiations, but He chooses, in most instances, to work through you and me.

"Why does God let evil and pain so flagrantly exist, even thrive, on this planet?" asks Philip Yancey in *Disappointment With God*. "Why does he let us do slowly and blunderingly what he could do in an eye blink?" Answering his own question, Yancey goes on to say that God does it for us, so that we can be developed.[3]

It had been a little over two years and I felt that I had developed. I had acquired a certain amount of understanding. I had broadened my interests, expanded my activities, improved my attitude on life and boosted my shattered self-esteem. I was making real progress, I believed, and then the invitation to the annual retirement dinner for the College arrived. This was the year W. C. would have been among the honorees.

Though I felt very comfortable with where I was in the grief process, I was apprehensive about opening wounds again, exposing myself to memories and longings that I knew would be painful. I suppose that this was the day I had dreaded above all others. No official mention was made of W.C. but most of his colleagues had a hug, a few tears and comments regarding how much they missed sharing this night's festivities with him. It brought back the whole unresolved issue of retirement years.

We had planned to set aside a block of time in which to travel, rediscover each other and establish a meaningful, but somewhat less hectic, routine for this phase of our lives. Memories were all I had left, but they were blessed, beautiful and bountiful and they refused to be pushed aside or minimized. I was beginning to experience peace and joy through them.

I prayed for strength to release all vestiges of resentment I continued to feel at the thought of those lost years. "Oh, God, I still don't understand why; he was such a good man," I whispered. Then I realized the absurdity of that statement. He *was* a good man, and even good men die. Death comes to all of us at one time or another, and I could rejoice that he was enjoying the rewards of a life well lived. It was I who was hurting without him. I was the one who needed God's strength to go on until I, too, would be a part of His eternal life. I felt that strength and I knew that in time this longing for lost opportunities would lessen. Perhaps it would never go away completely. It was probably something I'd have to live with. Whenever this longing hit me, and it did from time to time, like a ton of bricks, I'd call forth the projects in which I used to find great fulfillment. I'd select the one that was most appealing at the moment and dig into it. Perhaps it was bringing to life a new story character or polishing up an old manuscript. It might have been straightening out a closet or a drawer, or, heaven forbid, tackling the office I had allowed to pile up unmercifully. It might even have been paying bills, not a favorite pastime, but one that can get you into trouble if left undone.

Has God abdicated His position of power? Wouldn't it be reasonable for Him to wash His hands of someone who continues to feel resentment over lost dreams? Oh, no. God enables us to grow through the tragedies that come into our lives. He is with us in our time of need, suffering as we suffer, hurting even more than we hurt, grieving as we grieve. He doesn't promise us it will be easy, but He does promise us strength beyond our wildest expectations. He empowers us to take each small step. He helps us weigh our options and make important decisions as we go about the daily tasks of rebuilding our lives.

Rebuilding my life had been the focus of my every waking moment. It had become easier to face each new day because I knew that God would be there for me, but I began to take that for granted. I had become preoccupied with claiming this new existence for myself, preoccupied to the extent that I began to lose sight of my priorities. Because God knows our every thought and action, I'm sure He wasn't surprised to hear the following confession. In fact, I am certain that I was much more surprised than He.

"We have been traveling through this maze for two years and eight months now, God. We have skipped some steps and intermingled others as we climbed toward the goal of complete healing. That goal may never be reached, but I marvel at the progress we have made. And now, much to my chagrin, I am becoming lax. My searing pain no longer drives me to seek Your presence constantly and I find myself drifting off to sleep in the middle of my prayers—or worse yet—forgetting to pray at all. Like so many times in my life, when the crisis has abated, I resume normal living. Forgive me, God, and help me to honor the time I have set aside for communion with You and the study of Your word. Help me to continue to come to You with a spontaneous 'thank you,' a word of praise or a petition for help, not only for myself, but for others who are also in need of Your presence."

I didn't want to lose the closeness with God that this grief experience had engendered. I didn't want to forget the gifts of personal salvation and immortal life that He, through His son, Jesus Christ, had given me. Neither did I want to harbor the doubts that occasionally crossed my consciousness.

How can Heaven hold all of the people who have lived through the ages and still have room for the thousands who die each day? And what about those who have yet to be born and will die in the ages to come? How will I be able to find my loved ones who have gone on before me? Will I recognize them in their spiritual bodies, just as the followers of Jesus finally recognized Him when He appeared to them after His resurrection? Is it simplistic to feel that I will be transported into God's presence and into the presence of my loved ones at death? Can I dare hope that they will be there to help me over the threshold?

What is Heaven like? Will we have a special relationship with those we had a special relationship with here? I can't bear to think of giving that up. And what kind of work will there be to do? W. C. would be so unhappy to "rest in peace" for eternity! Believe me, if he doesn't have meaningful work, there will *be* no peace!"

HAS GOD ABDICATED HIS POSITION OF POWER?

Bishop Hunt talks about a conviction that has developed significantly in his thinking during recent years regarding "the continuing individual growth and creative service in God's better world." He says, "I no longer simply welcome the concept of a heaven as a place of pure rest because my joy and fulfillment, both temporal and eternal, seem more dependent upon meaningful accomplishment."[4]

Can we communicate on a deeper personal level once we are reunited? Is W. C. ministering to the needs of family and friends as he ministered to them on earth? Is he hobnobbing with famous historical figures? How is his relationship to God manifested?"

Where is heaven? Is this all too complex and mind-boggling to be real? I don't want to harbor these doubts and with God's help I won't! Deep down I believe; deep down I know that all things are possible and that God is not limited. Deep down I realize that I see with human eyes and imagine with less than perfect insight. I know that I must trust God to carry out His plan in His own way. And so I push the doubts aside. I believe them to be a normal process of an inquiring mind and my mind, through faith, is satisfied. I'm glad that God has the patience to stand by me, even when I let Him down.

Has God abdicated His position of power? Wouldn't an all-powerful God strike out at us when we lose the way, when we falter, when our faith wavers? I think not. God doesn't force us to come to Him. He offers us this choice; He longs for us to accept, but He doesn't demand. Neither does He reject us when we strike out at Him. He gives us another chance, and another, and another.

Catherine Marshall's portrayal of God in her book, *Beyond Our Selves*, is delightful. She says, "God deals differently with each of us. He knows no 'typical' case. He seeks us out at a point in our own need and longing and runs down the road to meet us."[5] What a vivid depiction—what a glorious encounter—we don't even have to meet him halfway.

Though God is capable of intervening directly, and we can all cite examples when He has done so, our faith in an all-powerful God should not be dependent on this kind of intervention. God has not abdicated His position of power. No, a thousand times no! He has simply delegated that power—entrusted it to His children so that they may have the fullness of life He envisioned for them. Can we be less than good stewards of this amazing gift?

And, while we aren't obligated to meet Him halfway, imagine the joy of running up that road to embrace and to be embraced.

CLOWNING AROUND AFTER THE WEDDING OF
TWO DAUGHTERS WITHIN THREE MONTHS!

CHAPTER XV

Embracing Widowhood

"With God all things are possible."
(Matthew 19:26)

OR a long time I had steadfastly refused to think of myself as a widow, but I was finally comfortable with that word. This was curious. Oh, how I had shuddered when I first heard the term used in relation to me at W. C.'s funeral. I *can't* be a widow; that only happens to other people, I thought. But there I was, sitting with hordes of family and friends, my husband's lifeless body in a casket a few feet away. I knew that I no longer had a husband; I just wasn't ready to think of myself as a widow. I don't know why.

For the past few months, however, I had been thinking about what I called the chronological stages of widowhood. While I was careful not to refer to myself as a young widow, because my age would belie that, I found myself thinking in those terms. I likened the stages of widowhood to the stages of growth and development of a child and I found many similarities as I thought back to my own childhood and to that of my children and grandchildren.

Chronological Stages of Widowhood

Stage 1—*Dependent Infancy*

I didn't remember my own infancy, but I remembered that stage in my children and grandchildren and the children of my friends. They were dependent on the adults in their life for love, for basic care, for physical sustenance. The first stage of widowhood that I had gone through was remarkably similar. The warmth, the love, the hugs, the embraces had been crucial. They had helped me go on when I wasn't at all sure that this was possible. I sat back and let friends take over, providing for my family and me, even to the food that was put on the table. They knew what we needed, and they also knew that at that point in time I wasn't capable of providing for our needs. I accepted their care gratefully.

Stage 2—*Fledgling Youngster*

As a young child I had learned how to help myself, but I was still dependent on others to a certain extent. My friends were important to me and I counted on them to include me in their circle. At the same time, I wanted the opportunity of directing my own activities. I likened this stage of widowhood to the fledgling youngster, striving for autonomy. I was trying to put stability back into my life, to take on the responsibilities that were mine, and at the same time, I was grateful that my friends continued to offer me opportunities for fellowship and for a caring relationship that accepted me as I was at any given moment.

Stage 3—*Restless Youth*

As I grew older I took on the restlessness of youth and the longing for that elusive something that would make sense of my world and bring it all together. Widowhood's restlessness was every bit as intense and as intrusive, its need to make sense of a world gone awry as demanding.

Stage 4—*Responsible Adulthood*

And then I entered adulthood, that marvelous time in my life when responsibility, love, dedication and meaning became ever-increasing avenues of peace and fulfillment. Widowhood also had an adult stage. I had reached out for its comfort and support and I was beginning to experience its peace and fulfillment. As in the other three stages, the awareness of God and the assurance of His presence were abundant.

Letting go of my marriage was the first significant accomplishment of this stage of my widowhood. It represented great struggle, but I felt that this goal had finally been realized. Though many widows and widowers who reach this point in their grief process begin now to contemplate remarriage, I continue to view this as something that will probably not be a part of my experience. I don't rule out the possibility—only the probability.

If I fell deeply in love again I would welcome the intimacy and companionship. I would enjoy the belonging and freedom from loneliness. I would anticipate spending the rest of my time on this earth with someone who is compatible—someone who likes the things I like, holds similar values, strives for the same goals. I would enter the give and take of determining whose home to live in, what church we attend, how we would spend our money and bequeath our resources. I would do everything in my power to help both of our families become an integral part of our new relationship. I would even be willing to give up the freedom I now experience to take on the responsibilities of that new union. I would lovingly care for my spouse in sickness and health and would anticipate with pleasure receiving that same kind of care in my remaining years—if I fell deeply in love again.

I would never marry for companionship alone. Neither would I expect the breathless, earth-shaking experience of young love—though that is certainly not impossible. The emergence of a deep and abiding love that manifests itself in respect, each for the other, would be an absolute necessity—if I fell deeply in love again.

I could never forget W. C. or the wonderful life we shared, but I would not marry again unless I felt that I could keep that a treasured part of the past. I would expect my new marriage to be different and would try not to make comparisons. I think, however, that I would fail in these endeavors, and, while I am happy for those widows and widowers who find this kind of experience anew, I, at this point in time, do not anticipate ever falling deeply in love again! And so, I continue to wear my engagement and wedding rings on my left hand and W. C.'s wedding ring on a gold chain around my neck. I probably always will.

But I have stopped prefacing decisions with the question, "What would W. C. do?" I emulate his ideas only insofar as they mirror my own. I have learned to trust my instincts and feelings again, to determine what is right for me in my present situation. I would not have been true to myself if I had parroted W. C.'s every thought, word and deed when he was alive. I can't do that after his death, either. But I can take from our life together that which is still appropriate for me and blend it with the new adventures that are becoming a part of my experience. My life is leading in other directions, and since I have asked God to show me the way, it behooves me to follow His leading. It helps to think of my changes in life as moving from one pastorate to another. There are new friendships to form, new opportunities for service, new traditions to establish, and new worlds to conquer. My destiny does not lie in yesterday's ashes. It lies just ahead and the prospects are exciting.

I belong to an "I" household now. The simple act of leaving W. C.'s name off of a card or letter has taken great effort, but has finally become automatic. I no longer deprive myself of eating out when I don't have a companion and, much to my surprise, I find that I can enjoy the experience.

I try to cook nutritious meals in bountiful enough supply to put some in the freezer. These come in handy on days when I am too busy to spend hours in the kitchen. I set the table so the meal will be more inviting and turn the television or radio on when there is no one with whom to converse. It is no fun to eat alone in complete silence.

Travel is beginning to be of interest and I am planning opportunities to include this in my schedule of activities that will help me live life to the fullest. Enjoying pleasurable pursuits as well as work will be my goal.

As I neared the third anniversary of W. C.'s death I took time to reflect on my situation. I still miss him terribly; I know that I always will. But the hurt is tempered. I am caught up in projects that have real meaning and bring great joy—joy that I believed would never be a part of my life again! They fill the hours with purposeful living and bring fulfillment. Instead of wondering how I can possibly get through the long day ahead, I find myself wondering how I can get everything done in just twenty-four hours.

My book, *Lots of Ways to Win*, is in the bookstores and I have been involved in readings and book signings. I want to finish this manuscript and start the process of searching for a publisher. I honestly feel that it has been a joint effort. Not only has God been my companion and mentor on this journey through grief, He has given me the insight, the knowledge, the courage, the faith—and yes, even the words! And He has shown me that nothing is greater than the power of Jesus Christ to help one survive the tragedies that come into one's life.

My benevolent God has kept me in His love and care. He has put meaning and purpose within my grasp. He has made me whole again. I am not the person I was some years ago when I thought my life was shattered beyond repair. I'm glad that God knew differently.

I have finally embraced widowhood, and have found in it a sense of well-being and contentment. It is not what I would have chosen; neither is it the stressful, devastating existence I once thought it to be.

Grief has been a process of growth—of tiny steps and great strides. I know that it will be ongoing. Our journey through grief has been grueling, absorbing, mystifying, electrifying and satisfying. And when it is over—in God's own time—I will join Him and my beloved family for that long-awaited reunion.

"Let not your heart be troubled; ye believe in God, believe also in me. In my Father's house are many mansions; if it were not so I would have told you. I go to prepare a place for you. And if I go and prepare a place for you, I will come again, and receive you unto myself; that where I am, there ye may be also." (John 14:1-3)

CHAPTER XVI

Thank You, God!

"For ye shall go out with joy, and be led forth with peace:
the mountains and the hills shall break forth before
you into singing, and all the trees of the field
shall clap their hands."
(Isaiah 55:12)

SAIAH'S imaginative prophesy of the exodus of the Jewish people from exile in Babylon depicts the joy that must have been a part of that experience. Can't you just hear the mountains and the hills breaking forth into singing and see the trees clapping their branches? What beautiful imagery.

I can identify with those making the journey from exile. And I can appreciate the jubilation they must have felt at finally being freed to go home. I, too, have been freed to "go home," and my home, despite the absence of my loved ones, has become a good place to be once more. I look around at the familiar surroundings and am grateful for my storehouse of wonderful memories. They will stand me in good stead when future regressions into grief momentarily threaten my peace and contentment. Watching elderly couples walk hand in hand on the beach or share tables for two at a restaurant still bring yearnings, but these yearnings will not jeopardize by newfound joy.

I no longer dwell on what might have been. I look forward, instead, to each new day and the opportunity it brings. There will continue to be ups and downs, but God will be by my side. Thank you, God, for Your abundant presence.

I look out at the beautiful world He has created and marvel at the awakening of new life. The grass that was brown and patchy a few weeks ago has now burst forth into a bright green carpet. Spring flowers have pushed their heads through the earth in spite of its cold, hard surface. And the trees are budding profusely with a promise of grandeur yet to come. I know that this is part of God's plan and I note the lessons contained therein. Thank you, God, for helping me discover and accept the new life that is also mine.

I remember with nostalgia the springtime experiences that were a part of my kindergarten classes so many years ago. I was as thrilled as the children when the chickens started pecking their way out of the shell. I was also proud as a mother hen, having made numerous trips in the middle of the night to turn those incubated eggs. When the butterflies emerged from their cocoons after the long months of hopeful vigil, the children *and* their teacher were overjoyed. I note these lessons also, and apply them to the grief process. Oh, the persistence of those chickens and the glorious transformation of the caterpillars. Thank you, God, for strength to endure and freedom to become.

I search the night sky and take time to reflect, to wonder, and to dream. I am grateful for these quiet times and the opportunities they bring for communicating with God. I gaze at the radiant stars, the bright moon and the shadows that are reflections of my daytime world and I thank God for solitude, for peace, for contentment, for the assurance of His Being.

I smell the fragrance of the honeysuckle, hear the calling of the birds to their mates and enjoy the rich, sweet taste of a vine-ripened watermelon. I feel the surge of sand between my toes as the ocean waves lap gently across my feet. The majesty and awareness of these things had been lost to me for a while, but I am glad that they are part of my experience again.

I enjoy the sunshine and tolerate the rain because I know that it takes both to bring forth the beauty of God's world, just as it takes both to journey through a grief experience and emerge intact. Thank you, God, for this awareness.

I am grateful for the written word and the world of music and art that feeds our souls and brings understanding to our hearts. Without them, the quest for healing would be substantially prolonged.

And, oh, God, I am so thankful for the restoration of my sense of humor. It is good to be able to laugh again, to experience the joy that comes with seeing the funny side of a situation and to remember my many years of sharing these precious moments with my husband.

To actually share moments with him is exhilarating. Rereading his letters, his sermons, and his funeral eulogies has helped me to do just that. I have been reminded of truths that have been a part of my knowledge for many years, yet had to become part of my experience before they became entrenched in my consciousness—"There is no comparison between Methuselah's nine hundred and sixty-nine years and Christ's thirty-three. The value of life depends not on its extent, but on its intent and content—not on its duration, but on its quality." Through his writings W. C. reaches out to me with encouragement, compassion and love.

And these, his words of wisdom, couldn't be better expressed. "When death comes to a loved one it is a crisis experience. We muster our courage to face it and find consolation in the love of family, the support of friends, the memory of our loved one, and the assurance of our faith." I had forgotten that W. C. said these things as he tried to help others face their grief experiences. But because they have now become a part of my own reality, I can identify with them and respond with a hearty Amen! Thank you, God, for the courage to delve into W. C.'s writings and for the wonderful feeling of closeness this endeavor brings.

What a blessing it is to experience meaning and purpose and to realize that the gift of life is something I cherish once more. To be able to rejoice in today and look forward to tomorrow is thrilling. Truly, God is in His Heaven and all is well with my world once again.

This is the happy spirit in which I approached Easter, three years after W. C.'s death. As the sun peeked from behind the distant mountains I silently praised God for the reality of the risen Lord. That afternoon I went to the cemetery and sat by the graves of my loved ones. I reflected on their lives and thanked God for each one. Oh, how grateful I was for the wonderful experiences I had been privileged to share with W. C.—and what beautiful memories I had of my mom and dad. I could have dreamed the rest of the day away right there, but I felt a compelling need to return to the chapel.

The voices of worship that had been part of the glorious morning service were now silenced, the majestic music stilled. Sunlight beamed through the stained glass windows and danced across the altar, leaving its beautiful pattern of vivid colors on the carpet below. In an attitude of prayer and thanksgiving I thought about the influence of this lovely sanctuary on my family. The very tapestry of our lives together had been woven within its stately walls. It had been the scene of our children's and grandchildren's baptisms and confirmations, our worship together, our family weddings and yes, even our funerals. I sat down and absorbed the beauty that surrounded me. Peace and contentment poured into my heart as I experienced, perhaps for the first time, the depth of sentiment W. C. had felt for this holy place—and I knew that I was on hallowed ground.

I lingered there for a long time and let the struggles and the triumphs of the past three years surge through my consciousness. But the struggles were taking a back seat as the triumphs forged their way to the surface. Hope, joy and gratitude bombarded my soul. Happiness and excitement filled my heart. Satisfaction reigned supreme—for I was experiencing all of God's promises in all of their glory and I knew, beyond a shadow of a doubt, that our pilgrimage had led us to the pinnacle of the mountain and we were planting the flag of victory on solid ground!

The words of the majestic hymn, "Because He Lives," by Gloria and William Gaither, burst into my reverie and the certainty that I could face all of my tomorrows without fear and with great anticipation suddenly engulfed me.

> "Because he lives, I can face tomorrow;
> Because he lives, all fear is gone; because
> I know he holds the future, and life is worth
> The living just because he lives."[1]

Thank you, dear God, for this triumphant victory!

---

[1]"Because He Lives." Words by William J. and Gloria Gaither. Music by William Gaither. © Copyright 1971 by William J. Gaither. All rights reserved. Used by permission.

SOURCE NOTES

INTRODUCTION

¹Kübler-Ross, Elizabeth, *On Death and Dying* (New York, New York: The Macmillan Company, 1969, Seventh Printing 1971), 34-122.

²_____, *On Death and Dying*, 122.

³Westburg, Granger E., *Good Grief* (Philadelphia, Pennsylvania: Fortress Press, 1989), 21-63.

CHAPTER I

¹Allen, Charles L., *The Greatest of These is Love* (Carmel, New York: Guideposts, 1986), 12.

CHAPTER II

¹Manning, Doug, *Don't Take My Grief Away* (San Francisco, California: Harper & Row, Publishers, 1979), 11-13.

²_____, *Don't Take My Grief Away*, 23.

CHAPTER III

¹Manning, Doug, *Don't Take My Grief Away*, 41.

²Diets, Bob, *Life After Loss* (Tucson, Arizona: Fisher Books, 1988), 133.

CHAPTER IV

¹Kreis, Bernadine and Pattie, Alice, *Up From Grief* (New York, New York: The Seabury Press, 1982), 119-120.

²Reccord, Robert E., *When Life Is The Pits* (Old Tappan, New Jersey: Fleming H. Revell Company, 1987), 177.

Source Notes

Chapter V

[1]Brown, Elizabeth B., *Sunrise Tomorrow* (Old Tappan, New Jersey: Fleming H. Revell Company, 1988), 21-22.

[2]Dunnam, Maxie, *Living The Psalms* (Nashville, Tennessee: Upper Room Books, 1990), 151, 136.

[3]Kushner, Harold, *Who Needs God* (New York, New York: Pocket Books, 1991), 175-176.

[4]Colgrove, Melba, Bloomfield, Harold H. and McWilliams, Peter, *How To Survive The Loss Of A Love* (New York, New York: Lion Press, 1976), 76.

Chapter VI

[1]Veninga, Robert, *A Gift of Hope* (Boston, Massachusetts: Little Brown and Company, 1985), 154.

Chapter VII

[1]Brothers, Dr. Joyce, *Widowed* (New York, New York: Simon & Schuster, 1990), 89.

[2]Kübler-Ross, Elizabeth, *Death—The Final Stages of Growth* (New York, New York: Simon & Schuster, 1975), 164.

Chapter IX

[1]Miller, William A., *The Joy of Feeling Good* (Minneapolis, Minnesota: Augsburg Publishing House, 1986), 176-186.

Chapter X

[1]Kaufman, Barry Neil, *Happiness Is a Choice* (New York, New York: Fawcett Columbine, 1991), 91.

Chapter XI

[1]Peale, Norman Vincent, *The Power of Positive Living* (New York, New York: Doubleday, 1990), 66-67.

SOURCE NOTES

CHAPTER XII

¹Shneidman, Edwin, *Voices of Death* (New York, New York: Bantam Books, 1980), 176.

CHAPTER XIII

¹Schuller, Robert H., *Life's Not Fair but God Is Good* (Nashville, Tennessee: Thomas Nelson, Publishers, 1991), 177.

CHAPTER XIV

¹Hunt, Earl G., Jr., *I Have Believed* (Nashville, Tennessee: The Upper Room, 1980), 91-92.

²Kushner, Harold S., *When Bad Things Happen To Good People* (New York, New York: Shocken Books, 1981), 80-85.

³Yancey, Philip, *Disappointment With God* (Carmel, New York: Guideposts, published by special arrangement with Zondervan Publishing House, 1988), 174.

⁴Hunt, Earl G., Jr.,*I Have Believed*, 161.

⁵Marshall, Catherine, *Beyond Our Selves* (New York, New York: Avon Books, 1961), 56.

WORKS CONSULTED

Allen, Charles L. *The Greatest of These is Love*. Carmel, New York: Guideposts, 1986.

Brothers, Dr. Joyce. *Widowed*. New York, New York: Simon & Schuster, 1990.

Brown, Elizabeth B. *Sunrise Tomorrow*. Old Tappan, New Jersey: Fleming H. Revell Company, 1988.

Claypool, John. *Tracks of a Fellow Struggler*. Waco, Texas: World Book Publisher, 1982.

Cramer, Kathryn D. *Staying on Top When Your World Turns Upside Down*. New York, New York: Viking Penguin, 1990.

Colgrove, Melba, Bloomfield, Harold H., and McWilliams, Peter. *How To Survive The Loss Of A Love*. New York, New York: Lion Press, 1976.

Deits, Bob. *Life After Loss*. Tucson, Arizona: Fisher Books, 1988.

Dodd, Robert V. *Out of the Depths*. Nashville, Tennessee: Abingdon Press, 1986.

Dodd, Robert V. *When Someone You Love Dies*. Nashville, Tennessee: Abingdon Press, 1986.

Dunnam, Maxie. *Living The Psalms*. Nashville, Tennessee: Upper Room Books, 1990.

Goodrich, Robert E., Jr. *On the Other Side of Sorrow*. Atlanta, Georgia: The Protestant Radio and Television Center, Inc. 1955.

Hunt, Earl G., Jr. *I Have Believed*. Nashville, Tennessee: The Upper Room, 1980.

Kaufman, Barry Neil . *Happiness Is a Choice*. New York, New York: Fawcett Columbine, 1991.

Kreeft, Peter J. *Love Is Stronger Than Death*. San Francisco, California: Harper & Row, Publishers, 1979.

Kreis, Bernadine and Pattie, Alice. *Up From Grief*. New York, New York: The Seabury Press, 1982.

Kübler-Ross, Elizabeth. *Death, The Final Stage of Growth*. New York, New York: Simon & Schuster, Inc., 1975.

Kübler-Ross, Elizabeth. *On Death and Dying*. New York, New York: The Macmillan Company, 1969, 1971.

Kushner, Harold S. *When Bad Things Happen To Good People*. New York, New York: Shocken Books, 1981.

Kushner, Harold S. *Who Needs God*. New York, New York: Pocket Books, 1991.

Lewis, C. S. *A Grief Observed*. New York, New York: Bantam Books, 1976.

Malz, Betty. *My Glimpse of Eternity*. Carmel, New York: Guideposts, published by arrangement with Chosen Books, 1978.

Manning, Doug. *Don't Take My Grief Away*. San Francisco, California: Harper & Row, Publishers, 1979.

Marshall, Catherine. *Beyond Our Selves*. New York, New York: Avon Books, 1961.

Marshall, Catherine. *To Live Again*. New York, New York: Manor Books, Inc., 1974.

Miller, William A. *The Joy of Feeling Good*. Minneapolis, Minnesota: Augsburg Publishing House, 1986.

Osis, Karlis and Haraldsson, Erlendur. *At The Hour Of Death*. New York, New York: Avon Books, 1977.

Peale, Norman Vincent. *The Power of Positive Living*. New York, New York: Doubleday, 1990.

Pennington, J. C. *Surviving the 90s*. Washington, D. C.: Potomac Publishing, 1989.

Reccord, Robert E. *When Life Is The Pits*. Old Tappan, New Jersey: Fleming H. Revell Company, 1987.

Ritchie, George G., Jr. with Elizabeth Sherrill. *Return From Tomorrow*. Carmel, New York: Guideposts, published by arrangement with Chosen Books, 1978.

Schuller, Robert H. *Life's Not Fair but God Is Good*. Nashville, Tennessee: Thomas Nelson, Publishers, 1991.

Shneidman, Edwin. *Voices of Death*. New York, New York: Bantam Books, 1980.

Tengbom, Mildred. *Letting Tears Bring Healing and Renewal*. St. Meinrad, Indiana: Abbey Press, 1990.

Vanauken, Sheldon. *A Severe Mercy*. New York, New York: Bantam Books, 1977.

Veninga, Robert L. *A Gift of Hope*. Boston, Massachusetts: Little Brown and Company, 1985.

Walpole, Margaret. *Walking Into The Morning*. Norwalk, Connecticut: The C. R. Gibson Company, 1986.

Weems, Lovett H., Jr. *Christian Funeral*. Nashville, Tennessee: Abingdon Press, 1986.

Westburg, Granger E. *Good Grief*. Philadelphia, Pennsylvania: Fortress Press, 1989.

Yancey, Philip. *Disappointment With God*. Carmel, New York: Guideposts, published by special arrangemtnt with Zondervan Publishing House, 1988.

If you would like to give a copy of ***TOGETHER WITH GOD*—A Journey through Grief** to a friend you can order directly from Granny Lavender Press. Please enclose $11.95 per copy (there are no shipping and handling charges). For credit card orders—Visa, Mastercard, Discover—please include your card number and expiration date. Va. residents need to add 54¢ sales tax per book. Send your order to:

Granny Lavender Press
33325 Graceland Lane
Glade Spring, Va. 24340